Remarkable Women of the Scriptures

David Schepps

Dorrance & Company • *Philadelphia*

Copyright © 1976 by D. D. Schepps
All Rights Reserved
ISBN 0-8059-2305-5
Printed in the United States of America

To my remarkable women—
Robbi, Jill, Bessie, and Alice

Contents

Introduction	1
Eve	3
Emtelai	9
Sarah and Hagar	11
Lot's Wife	21
Rebekah	24
Bashemath and Judith	33
Leah and Rachel	34
Bilhah and Zilpah	44
Dinah	45
Asenath	46
Jochebed	47
Bithya	50
Miriam	50
Zipporah	59
Women of the Tabernacle	60
Elisheba	61
Puah	63
Shelomith	63
Achsah	64
Deborah	66
Jephthah's Daughter	74
Job's Wife	76
Tamar	77

Naomi and Ruth	80
Manoah's Wife	90
Delilah	93
Hannah	100
Ichabod's Mother	111
Nazbat and the Slave Girl	112
Michal	115
The Witch of Endor	126
Abigail	129
The Woman of Tekoah	139
Rizpah	143
The Woman of Abel	144
The Harlots before Solomon	147
The Woman of Shunem	149
The Maid of Israel	156
Jezebel	159
Jehosheba	173
Huldah	177
Esther	179
Judith	197

Introduction

In the moral pageant of human struggle that is presented to us by the Old Testament, the place of women—Jewish women of every description—is integral. From the time of the patriarchs to the giving of the Law, throughout the Exodus, the Captivity, and the Diaspora, the significant role of women in Hebrew history has testified to the endurance, the forcefulness, and the multifaceted character of women down through the ages. It is both instructive and inspiring to review the careers of some of the Old Testament's great female figures, in this time of growing historical and spiritual self-consciousness among the women of the world.

The Old Testament, like all great literature, is a book which imparts its wisdom in the context of a full-bodied humanity coming to grips with itself and its beliefs. No pasteboard characters populate its pages, no one-dimensional natures vitiate its moral assurance. This fullness of vision lends to all its unforgettable personages, whether male or female, the resonance of actual human existence. Thus, specifically as regards women, the Old Testament presents a portrait of more complex femininity than one will find in most of the world's literature, either religious or secular. One thinks of Miriam as but one example of a character whose complexities are as terrible and real as those of life itself, for her goodness, faithfulness, and percipience are riven by an incontinent will and overpowering ambition. Moreover, Miriam possesses all the qualities of literature's great tragic figures: when God cruelly chastens her, she repents out of a hard-won awareness of her own difficult nature.

Miriam, of course, is not the only vivid and complete female portrait in the biblical gallery; the Old Testament abounds in stories of woman's courage as well as weakness, goodness and sin, intelligence and recklessness. Were the Old Testament to present a less than many-sided view of humanity, it would not seem so true to us, and would not be the great book that it is.

It seems incredible, then, that the old charge of female suppression was ever brought against the Jewish religion, as if the law of Moses had consigned the Hebrew female to the sloughs of degradation. Or as if she ever required the experience of Christianity to elevate and console her.* In point of fact, Jewish law exalted, protected, and provided for woman, not in a patronizing or imperious fashion, but in the way that all true religions affirm the existence and the dignity of their adherents. The spiritual breadth of Judaism is too far-reaching to allow the promulgation of a narrow sexist or slave mentality, and the pages of the Old Testament embody this richness of vision.

We may regard the Old Testament, therefore, as an illustration of the true equality of the sexes before the Mosaic law. For we find women in the Scriptures playing out their roles not only as wives and mothers, but as thinkers and prophets, warriors and lovers, leaders and comforters. We see in its pages all sorts of women, ordinary and extraordinary, and we contemplate in their characters both the sacrifice and the cruelty, the heights and the depths, of which humankind is capable. And as the justice of the Hebrew God falls equally upon all, regardless of station or sex, so the Old Testament, as the supreme literary example of the Jewish moral system, treats all equally in its harsh, beautiful, and ennobling spirit.

I have included in this work biographies of both major and minor female characters, ordered in terms of the rough chronology in the

---

*See, as regards this familiar assertion, the introduction to Jean de Fraine, *Women of the Old Testament*, trans. F. L. Ingram (De Pere, Wisconsin: St. Norbert Abbey Press, 1968), pp. 3-4.

Old Testament, from the age of the patriarchs all the way through to the kingdom and dispersion. Major characters, such as Rachel and Esther, are, of course, given more space than minor figures; but, in any case, I do not claim to have exhausted the subject.

If, by the example of these biographical sketches, I give some indication of both the literary and spiritual dignity accorded women in the Hebrew religion, then I will have gone some way towards the accomplishment of what I believe to be a pressing task.

Eve

"He planted a garden eastward in Eden, filling it with every tree that was pleasant for the sight, and good for food."

Thus, in the poetic words of the Old Testament, was earth created by God for the happiness of man. Nor was this all: endowed with capabilities of love, ecstasy, and wisdom, man still needed something more for the perfection of his joy. And God provided for that want.

"It is not good for man to be alone," God said. "I will make a helpmate for him." And thus woman was created, and brought to man, a being beloved above all others, whose qualities of sympathy and understanding should complement man's nature.

In the Jewish religion, all of creation had its origin in Love, whose purpose was perfect enjoyment. Love called out of a chaos a world teeming with life and beauty, so that sources of happiness might spring forth from nothingness. But woman's creation was a manifestation of love still greater than all which had gone before it.

Although the record of man's residence in paradise is mournfully brief, there is sufficient scriptural authority for examining Eve's innocent career. For she was placed in the garden with every capability of attaining fulfillment. She had all of nature to contemplate and the Almighty with whom to commune, and she possessed the kindred spirit of Adam as her lover and companion.

The spirit which God breathed into man when he became a living soul was the essence of the Godhead, enabling both Adam and Eve to commune with their creator in complete harmony. No dishonesty or fear could darken and so deaden spiritual joy. Nothing of doubt could stagnate love. For everything around and within them bore the impress of the Creator's hand.

Apart from the spirit which God gave to man was the mind, which opened to these creatures formed in His image the inexhaustible resources of wisdom, imagination, and knowledge—everything, in fact, that could generate that highest of all pleasures, mental joy. Sources of what is now termed wisdom, that is, books of study, were of course unknown to Adam and Eve; neither did they need them. For these biblical progenitors there was enough to excite and satisfy their mental powers, enough to inspire emotions of wonder and adoration. Their communion with the Creator, the tidings of spiritual hosts, the contemplation of nature, constituted knowledge in its purest and most advanced state.

Nor was spiritual and mental happiness Eve's only portion. Formed, like man, in the immortal likeness of the Creator, she was man's equal in his responsibilities towards God and in the care of His creatures. She and man were endowed equally but differently. His mission was to protect and to guide; hers, to soothe, bless, persuade to right, and help in all things.

It is a beautiful picture, one infused with the poetic transport that is at the root of all religions. We see in paradise a vision of utter harmony, of spontaneous bliss and serene order. And yet in this paradise events were to transpire of a sadly different nature. For God called into being two trees, differing in their beauty from all others in the garden. They were the tree of life and the tree of knowledge. Of the first so little is known that we might suppose its purpose to have been thwarted by the disobedience of man. At a later period we read: "Lest man put forth his hand, and take also of the tree of life, and eat and live forever..."; thus, we may conjecture that it possessed qualities far greater than those of the tree of knowledge. In any case, man forfeited his right to its tantalizing fruits.

Of the tree of knowledge, its intentions and uses, we have more than sufficient information. Apparently it was too slender and meaningless an existence, if man had no temptation to disobey, to rebel, to question. Though subject to God's will and deriving existence from His hand, and enjoying life and all its varied pleasures by dint of an infinite love, man was endowed with the power of free will. For God to guard man jealously against every temptation, to surround him with enjoyment, and thus to bring forth only gratitude, is not in accordance with the perfect economy of love which is expressed in the Old Testament. It showed a deeper love to permit man to win his immortality and eternal innocence than it would to bestow these blessings upon him unsought, and therefore little valued. Of course, Adam and Eve could be guilty of no crime in such a guileless paradise. They were, after all, the sole possessors of the newly created earth; they were in daily communion with their creator and therefore not involved with idolatry, blasphemy, Sabbath-breaking, dishonoring of parents, murder, adultery, theft, false witness, and covetousness. No, there was only one transgression that they could commit, and that was disobedience.

"And the Lord God commanded the man, saying, Of every tree of the garden thou mayest freely eat; but of the tree of knowledge of good and evil thou shalt not eat; for in the day that thou eatest thereof, thou shalt surely die." And the young Eve, secure in her innocence, went forth to that very tree.

Coiled at its root was a serpent, "who was more subtle than any beast of the field which the Lord God had made." The serpent told Eve that God was mistaken in his judgment of the tree, that she would not die by eating of its fruits—that, to be sure, the knowledge of good and evil was the knowledge of the gods. "And when the woman saw that a tree was good for food, and it was pleasant to the eyes, and a tree to be desired to make one wise, she took of the fruit thereof, and did eat; and she gave also unto her husband with her, and he did eat."

In these brief but emphatic words are detailed those incidents upon which the whole after-history of the Jewish moral world is founded. To disobey God, one's own nature, is the first sin, from which all others flow. For when she disobeyed, Eve's whole nature was changed. The seeds of frailty, of whose existence she had been but hardly conscious, sprang up into an overweening trust in her own strength, a desire to act alone, independent of all control, to become greater, wiser, more exalted than creation itself. "She took of the fruit thereof and did eat." For a brief interval perhaps, when first she tasted the exquisite fruit, the struggle between innocence and knowledge was stilled in a strange, fearsome intoxication of joy. She had broken all barriers, thrown off all bonds, and had acted by herself.

It is idle to speculate as to whether Eve gave the fruit to Adam to assuage her own guilt or whether Adam took it passively, out of love for her. It may be that he was quite as intoxicated as she, and for the same reasons. At any rate, the crime was consummated. They fell together.

With evening came remorse, and when God's voice reached them they went into the woods to hide. Terror banished joy, and in the place of love was guilt. "And the Lord God called unto Adam, and said unto him, Where art thou? And he said, I heard Thy voice in the garden, and I was afraid, because I was naked; and I hid myself. And the Lord God said, Who told thee that thou wast naked? Hast thou eaten of the tree, whereof I commanded thee that thou shouldst not eat? And the man said, The woman Thou gavest to be with me, she gave me of the fruit, and I did eat. And the Lord God said unto the woman, What is this thou hast done? And the woman said, The serpent beguiled me, and I did eat." God knew she had spoken the truth and proceeded to pronounce sentence upon them. "I will put enmity between thee and the woman, and between thy seed and her seed; it shall bruise thy head, and thou shalt bruise his heel." And the dust of which the body was composed was commanded to return to dust. Enmity, strife, and death—such was the punishment which they and humankind were to endure.

Eve's chastisement was perhaps more severe than her husband's, for now she was to be subject to Adam not, as before, out of the obedience of love but out of duty; and, as a mother, she was to be exposed to anguish unknown to men. As for Adam, he was cursed to work the earth in labor before the earth would yield her fruits. But as the result of this punishment, a new and sober love was to grow between Adam and Eve. A love not full of happiness but full of sorrow and repentance. A love to banish all the harshness and despair of their expulsion and to soothe them in their wanderings. Adam once more took Eve to his bosom, as the sharer of his toils and cares, just as he had once taken her for the completion of his happiness. But this very love—this recognizable *human* love, with its frailty, imperfection, and strange nobility—was only an indication, in fact, of the coarseness of the new world they were entering. For in Eden they had not needed to love in such a way; now this new, all too human love was their only defense against a desert waste that would render them precious little.

Their names are not mentioned again in the Bible, but events occurred which brought them once more to the forefront of the Old Testament narrative. And in these events Eve's motherhood, and the cruel pain of it, is cast into vivid relief. For she bore a son, Cain. "I have gotten a man from the Lord!" she cried, and experienced a joy with which not even Eden, perhaps, could have provided her. Cain—from the Hebrew word meaning "to possess" came that name—was Eve and Adam's fondest possession. Reared so as to know no sin, Cain did not return the love and reverence they heaped upon him. But by the name bestowed on Eve's second son, Abel—from the Hebrew word meaning "transience"—it can be guessed that these first parents were already feeling the vanity of their hopes and wishes. At any event, from boyhood Cain manifested a passionate, strong will, which led in later years to horrendous consequences.

In her motherhood, Eve experienced the old curse. Death, as concerned herself and her family, was still the dark uncertain shadow whose presence she could not comprehend. God prepared to reveal it, but through clouds of a denser, more appalling blackness than had yet gathered round His creatures. For, wrought up by the preference bestowed on his pious brother, "it came to pass, when they were in the field together, that Cain rose up against his brother Abel, and slew him."

Death was mysterious no longer. In its most fearful shape it had descended to earth—dealt by a brother's hand. Eve's agony was immeasurable, for she had, in effect, been deprived of both her sons at one stroke. She mourned not only for the innocent one, whose blood was shed, but for the other one as well, who was doomed to wander without the solace of his kind. She had reached for knowledge, and now found it to be sharp as a knife.

In Abel's death she saw the end of existence. But in Cain's punishment she saw death *in* life, for he was exiled forever from her sight, a wretched wanderer.

However, Eve bore her bereavement, and it was a testament to her strength that God gave her another son, called Seth. And from Seth descended a line of venerable patriarchs, one of whom was brought to God, without dying, for his righteousness; another of whom was Noah, who alone was saved from universal destruction; and another of whom was Abraham, for whose sake Israel was the chosen of God. In short, Eve was comforted by a son quite as righteous as her fallen Abel, quite as beloved as her wandering Cain.

Scripture does not mention the death of Eve. Adam, we are informed, lived eight hundred years after he had begotten Seth, and had many other sons and many daughters. Since we are not told that Adam took another wife—as was the case with the other patriarchs—them we may assume that this splendid longevity was given Eve as well. Whatever was intended on this point, it is evident that long life is at least *morally* necessary in the story of Eve. For it would take a long life to unravel the many implications of the Fall.

The knowledge of good and evil, which Eve, in her innocence in Eden, strained for, was to be amply afforded her in the long years after the expulsion. She was to see her husband toil for scant reward, when in paradise she had seen him fulfilled. She was to find reproduced in Cain the monstrous pride she took upon herself at the tree. In Abel's sad doom she discovered the vacuity of death, to which she had given not a thought in her time of innocence. But in Seth, and throughout the long contemplation of her progeny, she was to see the obverse of the coin, the good that is bound up with evil. She learned that though discord and strife and oppression and labor and care would reign on earth there was an all-pervasive love in the universe, a love that would so overrule the world that from transitory evil would come eternal good.

Had Eve been truly humble, she would not have sinned, it is true. But in atoning for her pride, she achieved the stature of a symbol—a symbol of the difficult human passage to virtue.

Emtelai

Presently we shall encounter the wife of the most revered follower of the "sole invisible God," but it behooves us, certainly, to pause for a moment in order to consider the remarkable mother of Abraham, called Emtelai, wife of Terah.

From Noah's time the earth had become soaked in blood, idolatry, and depravity. The implications of the Fall were still being unraveled in the inexorable march of the Old Testament narrative, and the hard lot of both men and woman profusely exemplified. The brief, wincing tale of Emtelai is one of the most affecting in all the Bible, and illustrates a kind of suffering peculiar to women, and a triumph peculiar to them.

Superstition had penetrated the earth, not the least among the family of Nahor, whose line shall be of such importance in the stories of the several woman who follow. Nahor's son, Terah, married Emtelai, a shy, simple, faithful girl. Their marriage, however, was blighted from the beginning, for Nimrod, the cruel king of Canaan, had read in prophecy that a babe was about to be born who would grow up to threaten both his power and his religion. This king decreed, therefore, that all pregnant women should be confined in one place, and all their male children murdered at their breasts, whereas the birth of female children should bring reward to the mother. What followed was, of course, a grave and horrendous slaughter of innocents.

Emtelai tried at first to hide her pregnancy, but her husband discovered it, and they were in great fear for the prospective offspring. But a miracle then occurred which signified the special providence attending their seed: though Emtalai was, indeed, delivered of a son, she was able to do so in secrecy, for not a sign of her pregnancy was ever visible on her body.

She had gone into the desert for this birth, for the babe could not be as miraculously hidden as her pregnancy. She went into a cave and there gave birth to Abraham (or Abram). And what followed is painfully illustrative of the plight of motherhood in those cruel times.

Emtelai lamented the futility of her plight, for she was faced with an awful decision. If she returned to her home, surely Nimrod would have the infant slaughtered like all the others. If she left him in the cave, he would die by the elements or be devoured by beasts. Her decision was heartrending: "Better thou shouldst perish here in this cave than my eye should behold thee dead at my breast." And there she abandoned him.

But when Emtelai returned to her home, she grew sick with yearning for her only child after twenty long and tortured days. Wildly she returned to the cave, and cried bitterly when she discovered that her babe was, in fact, gone—prey to beasts, she thought. Stunned with grief, she wandered out into the desert.

Years later, she encountered a strange man, to whom she imparted her sad story. She besought mercy of the heavens for having left her child so long alone, and was inconsolable until the man revealed that he was, miraculously, that abandoned infant, her son. Amazed, Emtelai inquired as to how such a thing could be. And Abraham told her of the "great, terrible, living, and ever-existing God," invisible and omnipotent. Meekly Emtelai asked if there was truly a God other than Nimrod. And Abraham replied, "Yes, mother, the God of the heavens and the God of the earth, He is also the God of Nimrod son of Canaan. Go, therefore, and carry this message unto Nahor."

Here, in one concentrated moment, was Emtelai to know both the agony and the pride of a mother's condition. Her own flesh had been torn from her, only to be restored to her whole, and larger than life.

And Emtelai returned and conveyed the message to her husband's father, from which issued, finally, the rage and ultimate chastisement of Nimrod. Her glorious message was imparted; the Old Testament narrative ends about Emtelai, mother of Abraham.

Sarah and Hagar

So significant are the incidents in the life of Eve, that, with a cursory look, Sarah's biography appears somewhat uninteresting. Still, as the partner of Abraham, Sarah is the subject of some reverence in the Hebrew religion; much of God's love and pity towards His creatures is revealed in her simple life, and also in the life of her bondwoman Hagar, which is closely intertwined with hers.

The real relationship between Abraham and Sarah, before marriage, has never been clearly established. Some commentators assert that she was his niece, the daughter of his elder brother; and others, that she was, as Abraham himself declares, his half-sister: "She is the daughter of my father, but not the daughter of my mother, and she became my wife."

These two are first called Abram and Sarai. The young wife accompanies her husband and Lot from the home of their people to a strange country, in obedience to the word of God. Scripture is miraculous regarding the young Abram, and his affectionate and virtuous conduct seems to have attracted the blessing of God and to have caused him to be chosen as the promulgator of the Divine

Revelation. It is very possible that Abram was exposed to many dangers because of his loving obedience to the "sole invisible God," instead of the idols of his race, and these dangers probably provoked the first removal of his family to Charran, where they seem to have dwelt in peace and prosperity, secure from persecutors. It must, then, have been hard to go forth again, without any definite cause for the removal.

Accompanied by Lot and their household—expressed in the phrase "the souls they had gotten in Charran," who were those they had instructed in the true faith—and carrying with them whatever substance they possessed, Abram and Sarai "went forth into the land of Canaan," which was inhabited by a fierce people who gave little hope of ever being converted by the patriarch and his family. Because of their constant journeyings, it appears that they could not even obtain sufficient land to fix their home. To add to their discomforts and trials, a famine broke out in the land, a famine so grievous that Abram sought the land of Egypt, where, fearful because of the beauty of his wife, he told Sarai to call herself his sister, not his wife.

But his fears were unfounded, and his substance increased in Egypt by Pharoah's gifts. He, Sarai, and their household retraced their steps to where "his tent had been at first, between Bethel and Hai." The altar which he had originally erected was still there, and again he and his family "called on the name of the Lord." The command of Pharoah—"Go thy way"—was most probably regarded and acted on by the patriarch as a warning, that his safest home was in the land to which God had originally guided him.

In the events which follow—the separation of Abram and Lot, the battle of the kings, the imprisonment and rescue of Lot, the blessing of Melchisedek—Scripture makes no mention of Sarai. Apparently her home was still an unsettled one. The Lord had again appeared to renew His promises to Abram, comforting him in the sorrow occasioned by Lot's dwelling in Sodom by the assurance that all the land which he saw, north and south, east and west, would be given him and his seed, and his seed's seed. Abram was told, "Arise, and walk through the land, in the breadth of it and in the length of it, for I will give it unto thee." Consequently, the tent of the patriarch was removed south to the plain of Mamre in Hebron, and an altar built at once to claim the land in the name of the Lord and to give his household a place of worship. The extent of the patriarch's household may be imagined when one considers the fact that, at his word, no less than three hundred and eighteen servants, born in his house and trained to arms, accompanied him to the rescue of his nephew. Those he left to attend his flocks and extensive herds must have been in equal proportion; and in his absence Sarai maintained dominion over them all.

Abram's warlike expedition was the only journey in which his wife did not accompany him. After the completion of the campaign, we have the first allusion to the patriarch's being childless. Evidently some doubts had interposed between Abram and his wife. Abram revealed his painful thoughts to his God: "Lord God, what wilt thou give me? Behold, to me Thou has given no seed." God had promised that the land should be his *and* his seed's, but Abram saw the years pass and still had not offspring. Presumably Sarai had long since passed the age when she could be a mother. To soothe this fear, the Lord promised that, as the stars, "so should his seed be."

Perhaps Sarai felt joy when this promise was made known to her. Her whole history proves that she was domestic and she may have often yearned for children. But any joy she may have experienced was of short duration. Sarai probably imagined that the fulfillment would immediately follow the promise. Finding that there was still no evidence of her becoming a mother, Sarai became subject to gloom, we may suppose, not only for reasons of frustrated maternity, but because she may have feared Abram's taking another wife, which was often the custom. After all, *her* name had not been mentioned as the destined mother of the promised seed. To forestall her own fears, and to insure the continuance of her husband's seed, Sarai had recourse to human means.

Most women in her position, influenced as she was by the customs of her time and place, and infused with the deepest affection and respect for her husband, would probably have both felt and acted as she did. The servant Hagar became Abram's second wife, at Sarai's own request.

The first intimation that Sarai's scheme would bring vexation and sorrow, as well as joy, was her disappointment with regard to Hagar's continued humility and submission. Forgetful that it was to her mistress that she owed the privileges of her sudden rank, the Egyptian, in her newfound pride, made known to all that Sarai was "despised in her eyes."

It must have been a bitter disappointment to Sarai that, instead of receiving increased gratitude and affection from one she had raised to such a position, she was hated by that one, whose insolence, if unchecked, might bring discord and misery in a household which had once been peaceful. Sarai was not a creature to submit tamely to ingratitude. There was neither coldness nor indifference about her.

Yet even this, an affair of feeling entirely between herself and Hagar, could not urge Sarai to actions unauthorized by her husband. Indignant, she no doubt complained to him of the secret fear that Hagar, favored by the prospect of impending motherhood, might be unduly protected and justified by the patriarch. But this was not so. Abram's answer to her entreaties and complaints at once convinced her that Hagar had not taken her place. Although Abram could not but feel tenderness towards the girl, he acknowledged Sarai's supremacy, both as his wife and Hagar's mistress, and told her, "Do with her what seemeth good to thee." We have too many proofs of Abram's just nature not to suppose that he felt his wife to be justified in her accusations. He knew, too, that she was not likely to inflict more punishment than was deserved, particularly on a favorite slave. Therefore, it was with Abram's full consent that "Sarai afflicted her, and she fled from her presence."

Whatever the nature of this affliction, it could not have been very severe, for Hagar had the power to fly. Reproof to a disdainful temperament is often felt as intolerable. And Hagar, feeling superior to all around her, must have had her pride deeply wounded by Sarai's reproaches, so that she took flight rather than submit. It was not until addressed by the voice of an angel that her rebellious feelings subsided.

For where was she to go, after all? Upon reflection, she must have seen the futility of her position, wandering in the wilderness all alone. Her former position must have become doubly attractive to her, as she headed she knew not where. She had resigned all the warmth and affection, privilege and joy, for the sake of her pride. Perhaps she was primed, by her own bitter reflections, for the voice of the angel.

The angel told her, "Return to thy mistress, and submit thyself to her power." In her awe, Hagar repented; and seeing that it was sincere contrition, the angel promised her that her seed would be multiplied so that it could never be numbered. It would not be Abram's promised seed, apparently, for nothing in his words implies it, but he assured her that God would not forget her son.

Thus did Hagar, the strong-willed and prideful servant girl, repent and return to Sarai. So much more forceful a character is Hagar that it is easily imagined how great must have been her repentance when she passively submitted herself to her mistress. Sarai, consistent with her biblical character, must have accepted her with full forgiveness. But neither divine speech nor sincere repentance was to completely eradicate the resentment between these two, and they were to be at odds again, Sarai wielding her stern claims. Hagar was sent wandering the earth once more. For though it is Hagar whom we think of as fiery, it must not be forgotten that Sarai, too, beneath her ingratiating domestic virtues, possessed a deeply passionate nature. But this is an observation which takes us ahead of our story.

For in due course the promise was fulfilled, and Hagar was delivered of a son, whom Abram, in his joy, called Ishmael.

For some years Abram and Sarai looked upon Ishmael as the promised seed. After a time, however, God again appeared to Abram and commanded him, "Walk before Me, and be thou perfect." In other words, Abram was now to be perfect in trust, in faith, and in deed, without any regard for strictly human probabilities. The patriarch's name was changed to Abraham, as befitting the many nations over whom he was to be father. The covenant appointed him and his seed as the chosen, the everlasting inheritors of Canaan, to act witness to God's truth. Furthermore, God desired Abraham to call his wife no longer Sarai, but Sarah: "And I will bless her, and give thee a son also of her; yea, I will bless her, so that she shall be a mother of nations; kings of people shall be of her." Thus, they were to be parents of many nations, not merely husband and wife to one another. Though swept away with amazement and joy, Abraham had still a thought for his existing seed: "O that Ishmael might live before Thee!" God soothed the father's fears by the promise that, though it was Sarah's seed with whom His covenant would be established, Ishmael would also be blessed and *his* seed multiplied so that, like Abraham, he would become the father of a great nation: "And for Ishmael I have also heard thee."

The acceptance of the covenant and the change in her own name was imparted to his wife, and to the household, with the additional information that Sarah, too, in her advanced age, would bear a son. Yet when the promise was repeated to her, Sarah dismissed it as a thing impossible to believe. Accustomed to thinking of Ishmael as the only seed of Abraham, Sarah's hopes of motherhood had long since vanished. Perhaps the promise, when first she heard it, dredged up too many painful feelings, which she had already subdued.

But events came to pass that brought the promise to the fore again. Engaged in her domestic duties, Sarah one day was interrupted by the hasty entrance of her husband, requiring her "Quickly to prepare three measures of fine meal, knead it, and make it into cakes." For visitors had arrived. Patriarchal hospitality was never satisfied by committing to hirelings the preparations fit for a hearty welcome. We see Sarah herself either making the desired cakes or superintending her domestics in doing so and the patriarch rushing out to fetch a calf from the herd, though he had plenty of servants around to save him the exertion. God had changed their names to indicate their innate aristocracy, and no scene illustrates better than this the refinement, nobility, and magnanimity of character in both the patriarch and his wife.

The primitive simplicity of the first Jewish fathers impresses upon us the idea that they were only farmers in a harsh land, but they were also princes and nobles with intellectual vigor and vast possessions. They had large and well-ordered households, lands adjoining their own establishments, and the respect and submission of those nations with which they came into contact. Abraham was always addressed as "My Lord," both by his own people and by other nations. He commanded others not only because of his inner strength and innate presence, but also because of the outward signs of privilege which he possessed—his lands, his herds, his domestics, and his army.

Yet, royal though Abraham and Sarah were, it was not in them to be aloof or artificial. In the Bible, nobility was nature and *heart*; simplicity and benevolence, cordiality and warmth. Neither coldness nor indifference could fold up their affections or thwart their feelings. Thus, when the visitors appeared, Abraham and Sarah prepared their welcome in a way characteristic of them, and they showed themselves to be royal indeed, in the true biblical sense. Sarah, no less than Abraham, prepared the meal as a mark of profound respect, which was a reflection of her majestic nature.

Sarah did not join her husband and their guests. The custom of the time precluded all intrusion, or even the wish to intrude. Unless summoned, the place of the Jewish wife was in the retirement of the home, not because of any inferiority of rank, but quite simply because economic roles so prompted. The ordered simplicity of the household affirmed both the place of the husband and that of the wife. It was always thus in ancient civilizations. Only in more modern and complex cultures have these roles been questioned and changed. But in biblical times, there was no economic diversification or upheaval to threaten the basic order of the household.

While seated in the inner tent, occupied with her usual duties, Sarah heard her own name mentioned among the guests. "Where is Sarah, thy wife?" asked one of the visitors of Abraham. He replied, "She is in the tent." The visitor responded with strange words: "Sarah, thy wife, shall bear a son."

Sarah was incredulous, naturally enough. Nearly twenty years had passed since the first promise of an heir had been given. Years full of incidents conducive to forgetfulness in regard to the promise. She supposed it fulfilled by Ishmael's birth. The covenant, too, as imparted to her by her husband, she had not believed. But soon the words of the visitor seemed a prophecy and a bright beacon, diminishing the forgetfulness and bringing new hope to her. She may well have regretted that she had not waited, had not believed, from the time when the promise was first made.

Before the birth of Isaac, however, Abraham and his household once again removed their dwelling, in consequence of the vile appearance and poisonous vapors of the once beautiful valley of Sodom. Again Abraham passed off his wife as his sister, out of fear for her safety—an odd fear now, since Abraham had, after all, made his covenant with the Lord, and was in His hands. For many years his life had been ordered and guided according to a special providence, and he ought to have known, perhaps, that all his fears were groundless.

Sarah herself was ignorant of the fact that her beauty had been supernaturally renewed. She even neglected to wear the veil, as is the tradition with Near Eastern wives even today. This neglect explains, perhaps, Abraham's misgivings; it certainly explains Abimelech's present of a "covering for the eyes," and the words "thus she was reproved." Her beauty subjected her to much danger, just as it had in her youth.

Miraculously protected by God, and publicly vindicated from all dishonor by the King of Gerar, Sarah and her husband continued to live in Abimelech's dominions. Here it was that at the appointed time "God visited Sarah as He had said" and the promised seed, Isaac, was born.

The very character of Isaac—meek, yielding, and disinclined to enterprise—indicates the lavish affection heaped upon him by his parents. "The child grew and was weaned," Scriptures tell us, "and Abraham made a great feast the day Isaac was weaned." Sarah's joy is easily imagined; she had waited so long for the child that the fierceness of her love was nearly a foregone conclusion.

But the weaning feast which Abraham gave was an occasion for sorrow, too. For Hagar and her son had been under the impression always that theirs constituted the promised seed. So Ishmael derided Sarah's maternity at the feast, and spoke disrespectfully of the child. Ishmael's youth, and Sarah's request that the bondwoman, too, be expelled, leads us to the supposition that it was Hagar who instituted the affront. It was, in any case, in Ishmael's interests to dispute the legitimacy of Isaac, and certainly not in human nature to let go the opportunity. But no other offense could have worked so on Sarah. So Hagar and her young son were expelled from their home and sent to wander the desert. They present a spectacle of some sympathy and consideration. By comparison, Sarah seems jealous and unduly harsh.

To be certain, on a superficial reading, Sarah does appear in a comparatively unfavorable light, as if she had been seeking the first opportunity of expelling Hagar and her son's rival. But then, it must be remembered that God Himself desired Abraham to hearken to the voice of Sarah in all she should say, for in Isaac *was* the promised seed, though Ishmael, too, would father nations.

Now, we know that Hagar had once been Sarah's favorite slave; but surely such a relationship could not survive the first falling-out, even though Hagar's contrition and Sarah's forgiveness had contributed to at least the appearance of amity in the household. And as long as both believed Ishmael to be the chosen seed, then the appearance was maintained. But with the birth of Isaac all the old animosities arose again. For one as affectionate as Sarah to have regarded Ishmael as her son for so long and not to have loved him is fairly improbable; but surely she did not love him as Hagar must have. And it must be remembered that Hagar was always an either active or dormant threat to Sarah.

In this painful tangle of familial relationships, Sarah's words cut through every strand: "Expel this bondwoman and her son; for the son of this bondwoman shall not inherit with my son, even with Isaac."

Now, Abraham's possessions were sufficient for the heritage of both his sons; still Sarah's angry words should be considered. After all, the course of nature had been reversed, and the younger, not the elder, was to be heir to the promise. Inevitably, discord and confusion would have ensued, and the brothers would have been continually at war. There was insight in Sarah's anger; for it was necessary that Ishmael form his own nation. It was harsh, and yet ultimately wise, that he should go into the desert.

Abraham, gentle and affectionate by nature, shrank from the

pang of separation, causing him to feel displeasure with Sarah for the first time in their long marriage. Yet when God spoke, it was obvious that this trail could not be averted. And Abraham knew that God would bring light into his son's darkness, for He had promised.

Readers are sometimes surprised at the small provision with which Abraham endowed his firstborn at their separation. But Ishmael was to become ancestor of a nation through the direct agency of God, and not through any provision made him by his earthly father. Abraham was acting in the spirit of the covenant.

The narrative of Hagar's wanderings with her son, of her maternal suffering, of her hardships and relief, is one of the most beautifully touching in the Bible. Now, Hagar was not of Abraham's race, but of that of Egypt; she was a bondwoman and a wanderer, exiled both from birthplace and her place of love in Abraham's heart; and she was now overwhelmed with anxious fears for her child, the only thing she had ever truly been able to call her own. She was in God's particular care, but He did not keep her from sorrow: "The water was spent in the bottle, and she cast the child under one of the shrubs, and she went and sat down over against him, a good way off, for she said, Let me not see the death of the child; and she sat over against him, and lifted up her voice and wept." Not until her trial was at its height did a pitying voice descend to soothe her. "What aileth thee, O Hagar? Fear not, for God hath heard the voice of the lad whence he is. Arise, lift up the lad, and hold him in thine hand, for I will make him a great nation." And the promise was fulfilled.

The whole history of Hagar is complex. She had an individual character of no little strength: she could be overbearing and insolent, affectionate and feeling. She was a sensuous, impetuous woman capable of great love for Abraham and searing hatred for Sarah. Given her time and circumstances, it is the force of her character that we remember, and not without respect.

Few other events mark the life of Sarah. God brought her safely through the anxieties of previous years, and fulfilled His promise. She lived many long years after the birth of Isaac, who loved her exceedingly.

And she was spared the great trial of the father. For she died before Abraham had to prove his faith in the sacrifice of their son.

Lot's Wife

"But his wife looked back from behind him, and she became a pillar of salt."

A short verse, a fifteen-word "biography," too insignificant, on the surface, to warrant our attention, since we are concerned with those female characters, briefly or lengthily drawn, as the case may be, whose presences make an indelible impression upon us. Here we have but the barest reference to a woman, almost an abstraction, without flesh or form. Yet the sentence symbolizes all that is of the flesh and of the passions; and the impression, historically, has been etched upon the Western mind.

The image of Lot's wife turning into a pillar of salt when she looked back at the city of Sodom is one that has inspired painters like Cranach and Rubens, and has furnished the equivalent of a moral apotheosis for scholars and poets through the ages. The evil we associate with the "cities of the plain," and the licentiousness of their inhabitants, so extreme that God's wrath poured down in fire and brimstone, comes to a head in the transformation of Lot's wife. It behooves us, then, to dwell upon this brief biblical verse, in order to draw out its many implications, especially in regard to womanhood.

Now, Lot was Abraham's nephew, and his character is not, in the Old Testament, represented by such sterling qualities that we may attribute much in the way of virtue to his household. For instance, when Abraham offered Lot his choice of land, the nephew greedily chose the most fertile portion. But even accepting the fact that Lot was no patriarch, may we judge the wife by the character of her husband? We can only assume, as she followed him unhesitatingly in his gravitation "towards Sodom," that she did not object to his tendencies.

More damning evidence of the woman's ill nature is provided by the account of her daughters' marriages to Sodomites, which bespeaks, at the very least, a shocking maternal carelessness. She could not have placed much importance on the strength of her line if she allowed her offspring to form such degraded unions.

Still, the evidence is all a matter of conjecture. Lot was a comparatively prosperous man, and we may assume that his wife was a proud woman, one desiring material possessions. That, at least, has been the judgment of her character in book and painting. So it is in conjecture that the meaning of Lot's wife lies, and in conjecture that we begin to understand something of her importance symbolically.

Whether or not she was corrupt is not important. The significance of the woman is shown by the connection we establish between materialism and evil. Though far removed from the circumstances surrounding the composition of the Old Testament, we continue to make this connection. We notice in Lot's wife, then, a tendency to shear away spiritual needs and obsessively, self-destructively, rivet upon the realm of material possessions and earthly objects.

Sodom, like Gomorrah, was a city whose sinfulness is not precisely defined for us in the Old Testament. It has a meaning beyond any *particular* sin; and has become for us a kind of receptacle for the run of soulless and jaded earthly pleasures. The Old Testament juxtaposes Sodom with the pristine integrity of Abraham's rural residences, far from the hectic, empty lusts of the urban environment. For a basically agrarian people, which the Jews were at this time, the city symbolizes loss of faith and sensual waste, a corrosion of the spirit that desiccates the character as finally and utterly as the salt into which Lot's wife turned. As we shall see again and again, in the stories of Dinah and Belilah, among others, the city was the fount of material excess from which man ought not to drink.

Evil women, like Delilah, or Jezebel, were products of the city. Perhaps the city, with its crowding and attendant ugliness, is naturally repugnant to man, especially agrarian man. In any case, the literary works of the ancient world, be they Hebrew, Greek, or Roman, paint the town as the place where religion and civilization finally decay. Women, as city denizens, are invariably cold and heartless, having only their own material interests in mind; whereas the householders and simple women of the hearth and field, like Sarah, for instance, think in terms of a greater good. We moderns may think of the rural areas as backward and crude—because we are industrialized men who cluster together in cities—but the ancient world had a much different view of the matter. The rural habitats of Abraham and the succeeding patriarchs and their wives, point up the grace and virtue the Old Testament attributes to honest labor performed in open fields and among pastoral flocks. Again, we are far from the days in which the Bible was composed, and no longer eschew the town, but we still carry with us the old suspicion that material accumulation is fraught with danger and will bring us low, should we overreach ourselves. Indeed, many members of the present generation are turning away from the cities, with their accelerated commerce and material trappings, to seek a purer existence in rural climes. And apparently they are not, like the wife of Lot, looking back.

The figure we are examining has, then, become associated with city women and with a yearning for self-aggrandizement and self-gratification. The emptiness of spirit which infected this woman, and forced her, against all warnings, to take one last lingering look at the city, is the emptiness against which the Old Testament repeatedly advises. For to mistake the object for the spirit becomes in the Bible a vicious "snare," as we shall see in the stories of women who lived in the period of Judges. Lot's wife is the first example we have of bad faith, by which people are drawn into a delusion as to the nature of the universe. The *things* which man creates for his own and others' profit are not the true substance of the cosmos, according to the Old Testament. Rather, man must use his creations for the good of others and for the glory of God. All must be consecrated by love for beings (and a Being) beyond oneself, so that objects do not evolve into icons and idols, to be worshiped for their man-made worth, in constant and loveless genuflection.

An interesting historical sidelight on the story of Lot's wife is provided by recent scientific investigations of the area surrounding the Dead Sea, where tradition has it that Sodom and Gomorrah stood. The Old Testament describes the destruction of those cities as a veritable rain of fire and brimstone. We may quote Mrs. Deen* in this regard, in order to illustrate the historical accuracy of the Scriptures, as a parallel to their moral accuracy:

> Geologists explain that at the south end of the Dead Sea is a burned-out region of oil and asphalt. A great stratum of rock salt lies underneath the Mountain of Sodom on the west shore of the sea. This stratum of salt, they say, is overlaid with a stratum of marl, mingled with free sulphur in a very pure state. Something kindled the gases which accumulate with oil and asphalt, and there was an explosion. Salt and sulphur were carried up into the heavens red hot. Literally it could have rained fire and brimstone. The cities and the whole plain and everything that grew out of the ground were utterly destroyed.

———— Rebekah ————

Abraham's kinsman Bethuel had a beautiful daughter, beloved and cherished by her parents and brothers; she, like Sarah, was given to the simple routine of domestic duty. It was to this girl that Abraham wished to marry his son Isaac. Her name was Rebekah.

---

*See Edith Deen, *All the Women in the Bible* (New York: Harper & Co., 1955).

There is no evidence in Scripture of her having ever been sought in marriage before the offer of Isaac. We suppose that she had scarcely been seen or known beyond the confines of her father's establishment.

The daily employments of the young women of Mesopotamia appear to have been completely domestic. Once, in the midst of her daily duties, Rebekah went, as usual, towards evening, to the well, with her pitcher on her shoulder, to draw water. A group of strangers stood beside the well with their camels. Perhaps, having lived in so circumscribed and protective a circle as that of her family, she was surprised at the sight of them; but if so, she did not show it, and went about the performance of her task. Rebekah had, even here, the serene temperament characteristic of the women of her station, whose simple duties were a reflection of an unchanging social order.

> And the damsel was very fair to look upon, a virgin, neither had any man known her: and she went down to the well, and filled her pitcher, and came up. And the servant ran to meet her, and said, Let me, I pray thee, drink a little water of thy pitcher. And she said, Drink, my lord: and she hasted, and let down her pitcher upon her hand, and gave him a drink. And when she had done giving him drink, she said, I will draw water for thy camels also, until they have done drinking. And she hasted, and emptied her pitcher into the trough, and ran again unto the well to draw water, and drew for all his camels.

The same artless nature that had led her to the quiet pursuance of her task also prompted the cordial kindness to the stranger, whose age won her respectful deference. She not only gave refreshment to the steward, but filled the trough for the camels to drink also. She must have gone up and back many times, from the well to the trough, with a weighty pitcher on her young shoulders. There were strong men about, but they were strangers and travelers, and she was in her own land.

Eliezer, the steward, wondered at her, and inwardly inquired of the Lord whether his journey had not, indeed, been worth the effort. For he was Abraham's emissary, come to fetch a bride for Isaac.

And here was the lovely object of his mission, as unpretentious and kind as could possibly have been envisioned. But he was anxious to make certain, and asked whose daughter she was, and whether her father's house might provide him and his fellows shelter for the night.

Rebekah replied, "I am the daughter of Bethuel the son of Milcah, which she bare unto Nahor." Furthermore, she said, "We have both straw and provender enough, and room to lodge in."

This little conversation between them took place, no doubt, while the camels were drinking; and when they had done, "the man took a golden earring of half a shekel weight, and the bracelets for her hands of ten shekels weight of gold." The maiden marveled not only at their richness but at the offer of them. True to her young and simple nature, she straightaway dashed off and "told them of her mother's house these things."

Now, it would appear that Rebekah's father, Bethuel, had passed away, for it was her brother, Laban, who, when she showed him the presents, went back to the well to inquire of the strangers. Evidently, the influence of Abraham's "sole invisible God" had penetrated even the far-off realms of Mesopotamia, where the patriarch's once hostile family resided, for Laban addressed the strangers as "blessed of the Lord." He told them that the house was being prepared for their visit and that provisions were being made for the camels. "And the man [Eliezer] came into the house, and he ungirded his camels. And they gave straw and provender for the camels, and water to wash his feet, and the men's feet that were with him. And they set meat before him to eat: but he said, I will not eat, until I have told mine errand. And he [Laban] said, Speak on."

As Laban had executed his duties as host, now the servant of Abraham, for his part, performed his. Earnest, faithful in heart and mind, Eliezer refused all food until he had delivered himself of his message. Having identified himself as Abraham's emissary, he told them the wondrous tale of how his master had grown rich and great by the blessing of the Lord, who had also granted him in his old age a son, to whom Abraham had given all that he had. He told them further how anxious Abraham was to guard his son from a connection with Canaanites, and to take him a wife from his own kindred, overruling Eliezer's own objection— "Peradventure, the woman will not follow me"—with solemn assurance: "The Lord ... will send His angel before thee, and prosper thy way." He told them how in obedience he had set forth, and, having arrived that day at the well, had prayed to the Lord of his master to grant that the virgin who, when he wished for drink should reply, "Drink thou, and I will draw for the camels also," should be the maiden whom he had been sent to find. Then he told of how his prayers had been answered by the appearance and kindness of Rebekah, and he concluded, "I bowed down my head, and worshiped the Lord God of my master Abraham, who had led me in the right way, to take my master's brother's daughter for his son. And now, if you will deal kindly and truly with my master, tell me; and if not, tell me; that I may turn to the right hand, or the left."

It was an affecting tale, that the rich, princely Abraham had remembered and yearned towards his father's house, seeking from them, in preference to all others, a wife for his son. "The thing proceedeth from the Lord," was their reply. "We cannot speak unto thee bad or good. Behold, Rebekah is before thee, take her, and go, and let her be thy master's son's wife, as the Lord hath spoken."

One night only the steward accepted the hospitality of his hosts. Anxious to report the success of his mission, he entreated, "Send me away to my master." But natural ties were not so quickly severed without pain. Rebekah had, after all, been the darling of the household; it was difficult, then, to send her off at once, because they might never see her again. "Let the damsel abide with us a few days," her mother and brother entreated in their turn, "at least ten; after that she shall go." But the steward pressed them to hinder him not, believing that to loiter would be displeasing to the Lord who had prospered his way. And they said, "We will call the damsel and inquire at her mouth." As young as she was, and unused to making great decisions, it was her voice that decided the matter: "And calling her, they said, Wilt thou go with this man? And she said, I will go." It was a brief and simple answer, yet suited alike to her character and the occasion.

Having accepted the presents of betrothal already, Rebekah would not detain the emissary of her new family. So her own house "blessed Rebekah, and said unto her, Thou art our sister; be thou the mother of thousands of millions, and let thy seed possess the gate of those which hate them." And Rebekah rose and, with her attendants, sought their camels and accompanied the steward on his homeward journey.

Canaan was reached at last, and the tents of the patriarch were in sight. Lifting up her eyes, Rebekah beheld a man walking forth in the fertile fields, bearing himself in a pensive fashion. The maiden probably guessed who it was, but when the question was asked of her guide, and he replied that it was Isaac, she alighted from her camel and, in her modesty, took a veil and covered herself.

She knew her own dignity. She demanded no more respect than she paid herself. She did not wait upon ceremony, but by shrouding herself in her veil she proved by this one action the respect due the son of Abraham, for she wished to conceal every charm until Isaac claimed her as his bride.

"Isaac brought her into his mother Sarah's tent, and he took Rebekah, and she became his wife; and he loved her: and Isaac was comforted after his mother's death." The emphasis upon Sarah's lingering presence in this passage gives some idea of the great love Isaac bore his mother, and of the close association of Rebekah's virtues with her own.

Neither presumption nor pride appear to have marked the conduct of Rebekah. The same steady performance of domestic duties, so evident in her girlhood, was to continue in her marriage. Every year she followed the quiet routine of daily chores.

Throughout these years the lives of Rebekah and Isaac passed peacefully. Abraham was still living, happy in his son's happiness. "Abraham gave [his other sons] gifts, and sent them away from Isaac his son, while he yet lived, eastward, unto the east country." Abraham knew that the promised seed was in Isaac, and therefore kept him near. Anxiously he, too, must have anticipated the birth that would prolong his line, but from his long personal experience in "waiting for the Lord," his fears were less intense than those of Isaac, who entreated the Lord "for his wife."

For twenty years Rebekah matured in the graces of womanhood. A beloved and cherished wife, daughter, and mistress of the household, her life passed by so smoothly, her affection so devoted to one object, that she was still entirely ignorant of the quicksand in her path which might bring her sorrow.

For example, when proof was given of God's grace in regard to Isaac's entreaty, her action was marked with the same childlike simplicity that had marked her in Mesopotamis. She went straight to her God, and lay to rest her own doubts. She asked no advice and demanded no help, but laid before him her emotions and asked him for a reply. The Lord told her that she was to be the mother of two opposing nations, one of whom should be stronger than the other, and that the "elder should serve the younger"—a strange mirroring of Isaac's own past. These mysterious words satisfied Rebekah, and she spoke not a word, neither of wonder nor complaint.

It is worthy of remark that Rebekah's is the first recorded instance of woman's immediate appeal to God.

At last Isaac and Rebekah became parents, first of one son, then of another. These children grew and flourished, but in early youth displayed a disparity in their temperaments and pursuits. Surely, with the words of God still in her mind, Rebekah could not have been surprised by the difference; still, though the prophecy had been fairly explicit, it had not *named* the chosen son. But Rebekah had begun to develop certain meddlesome tendencies, and from the first she favored Jacob, the younger son.

Because of our knowledge of Rebekah's innately kind and modest nature, especially as displayed in her youth, we require an explanation of these tendencies. Certain Victorian commentators* saw in Rebekah's actions at the well a forwardness, an overweening desire to please, that led directly to her presumptuous attitude with respect to God's words and the fate of her youngest son. After all, it was as if she were *nudging* providence, like a worrisome harridan, by so strongly favoring Jacob; and as these tendencies were, in time, to

---

*See, for example, Harriet Beecher Stowe, *Woman in Sacred History* (New York: J. B. Ford and Co., 1873).

lead her to alarming extremes, it is tempting to read into her youth some evidence of audacity. But in the Bible itself we see only that Abraham's most trusted steward—a man of no small percipience, evidently—considered Rebekah to be a sincerely gracious girl. Rather, we might seek our explanation in the childlike simplicity of Rebekah. For God had spoken, and she had absorbed His words at face value. She may, in her literal way, have misread the prophecy as a command, and acted accordingly. It was, I think, a case of believing in her God not too much, but in the wrong spirit. She had not Abraham's hoary wisdom, and Sarah's restraining influence she had never known.

In the next revelation after the birth of their sons, which was given to Isaac, God spoke expressly of "thy seed" in promising Isaac that nations would multiply after him. Thus, Isaac was justified in supposing that *both* his sons were concerned in the promises, until, of course, the eldest, Esau, disregarded his birthright. The fact that Isaac was not informed by Rebekah of the prophecy of the elder's serving the younger is indicative of the wife's literal-mindedness in taking the prophecy as a command.

Isaac, for his part, favored Esau. Probably he loved Esau better than Jacob because the boy was, in every respect, his opposite. Isaac was faithful, quietly and contentedly dwelling in one place, moving only at the command of the Lord, satisfied with the temporal and spiritual blessings which were his. Esau was bold and enterprising, roving about in search of active pursuits, heeding nothing but the moment, scorning homely ties, rude, rough, though capable of deep affection for his father. He was a hunter who brought Isaac's favorite meats to the table and who roamed far and wide in his adventures. Considering the complexities of the heart, it is understandable that Isaac should prefer Esau to Jacob, who was more like himself—"an upright man, dwelling in tents."

Partiality leads naturally to injustice, and in this regard it will be seen that Rebekah's favoritism was more intense than Isaac's. To Esau the balm of a mother's love was unknown, and, though his hasty marrige to the daughters of the Hittites was a grief to Isaac and Rebekah, the wife's neglect of her eldest son may have had much to do with Esau's reckless behavior.

While his sons were growing, Isaac's riches very greatly increased. A famine had sent Isaac and his family, by direction of God, to Gerar, and there he dwelt until he became so rich and mighty that the "Philistines envied him." Their king, Abimelech, told Isaac, "Depart from us, for thou art much mightier than we." And Isaac did so, and, after wandering for a time, fixed his tent at Beersheba, where the Lord again appeared to him, saying, "Fear not, for I am with thee." Beersheba, then, appears to have been the scene of all the events which followed— Esau's selling his birthright; his subsequent marriage; the vexations this action caused Isaac and Rebekah; and the infirmities of Isaac, which caused him to call his eldest back, so that he might "bless his son before he died."

Rebekah heard the words of her husband. She heard him call his firstborn to his couch, so that he might bless him before death robbed him of a reconciliation. Esau? Was Esau to have his father's blessing? He who had sold his birthright and spurned his privileges as heir? Rebekah could not accept it. And besides, how could the Lord's words be fulfilled in that way? She must prevent this thing and secure to Jacob the blessing. It would be easily accomplished, and surely, as the Lord had said it, she was justified in using any means necessary to bring it to pass. Such was her reasoning; she was urged on by a mother's love, and by a misunderstanding of the Lord's words.

Acting quickly, Rebekah called Jacob and informed him of his father's request. Fearing that with his upright nature he would shrink from the task she wanted to impose, Rebekah said, "Now therefore, my son, obey my voice according to that which I command thee." She claimed his unquestioning obedience before imparting her desire, and Jacob unwittingly agreed. When he heard her plan, however, Jacob respectfully and guardedly suggested that it was a fraud, and that it might bring upon him a curse instead of a blessing. Still Rebekah enforced the command, saying, "Upon me be thy curse, my son: only obey my voice." And he obeyed her.

The hands and neck of Jacob were disguised, so that their smoothness would not betray him, and thus attired to deceive, he approached the bedside of his blind father. "Come near, I pray thee, that I may feel thee, my son, whether thou be my very son Esau or not." And Jacob went close to his father, who felt him and said, "The voice is Jacob's voice, but the hands are the hands of Esau." And again, as if still doubting, Isaac asked, "Art thou my very son Esau?" Jacob answered, "I am."

"And it came to pass, as soon as Isaac had made an end of blessing Jacob, and Jacob was yet scarce gone out from the presence of his father, that Esau his brother came in." An interview follows that, for its pathos, is unsurpassed in all the Bible.

Rebekah, it is obvious, loved Jacob far better than his brother, but Esau was still her firstborn, and painfully must she have felt it when she heard his "great and exceedingly bitter cry." Esau asked, "Hast thou but one blessing, my father? Bless me, even me also, O my father; and Esau lifted up his voice and wept." Esau, the rude hunter, who had seemed to care for nothing but his pleasures, bowed down before his blind father and wept like an infant, beseeching the blessing of which a mother and a brother's treachery had deprived him.

"And Esau hated Jacob because of the blessing wherewith his father blessed him: and Esau said in his heart, The days of mourning for my father are at hand; then will I slay my brother Jacob. And these words of Esau her elder son were told to Rebekah." The mother, perhaps was more strongly moved by these events than she had thought possible; and her single-minded furtherance of what she conceived to be God's will only added to her sorrow. Crushed, she was forced to send her beloved Jacob away, for the sake of *both* her sons. "Behold, thy brother Esau, as touching thee, doth comfort himself, purposing to kill thee. Now therefore, my son, obey my voice; and arise, flee thou to Laban my brother to Haran." She attempted to make it seem as if it would not be for long that Jacob should stay away, but of course she knew it would be for a very long time indeed. She said, "Why should I be deprived also of you both in one day?" The cry implicit in this statement is that of sudden and chastening realization. God's mission, she knew now, was not *her* mission, nor hers to accomplish.

To Isaac she said, "I am weary of my life because of the daughters of Heth: if Jacob take a wife of the daughters of Heth, such as these which are the daughters of the land, what good shall my life do me?" It would have been extremely cruel to increase the troubles of the infirm Isaac by telling him of Esau's awful intentions towards his brother. Nor could the confession of her own fault in any way have redeemed matters. It would have excited Isaac's anger against her and would have caused him increased affliction. It was wiser to hide from Isaac the sad reason for Jacob's departure, and to do for his son what Abraham had done for Isaac. The father agreed and sent his youngest to "the house of Bethuel": "Take thee a wife from one of the daughters of Laban, thy mother's brother." And Isaac sent Jacob away. Thus was the mother parted from her favorite son.

With Jacob's flight, the history of Rebekah is concluded, for her name is no more mentioned. Even her death is not alluded to in Scripture. We do know that she was buried in the cave of Machpelah, according to Jacob (Gen. 49:30-31), but since there is no mention of her name upon Jacob's return, we must infer that she died before his arrival and never saw him again.

—Bashemath and Judith—

The two Hittite women who gave such "grief of mind" to Isaac and Rebekah were Bashemath and Judith, wives of Esau.

It is said that Esau wasted his substance in carousing and evil with the brothers of these women, and then married them in order to spite his own mother, as we have seen it so sadly told in Rebekah's tale.

Bashemath seems to have been instrumental in keeping Esau from his father's religion, and to have used her wiles to enslave him to Canaanite gods.

Judith bore Esau children, but his marriage to her was the

principal reason for his disinheritance. She seems to have been much less calculating than Bathemath, and more devoted to Esau's welfare, but no less hostile than her sister to the Hebrew God.

We see here examples of the authors of the Old Testament damning foreign women for idolatry, but straining—especially in the case of Judith—to see them as human beings following lights of their own.

Leah and Rachel

In Mesopotamia, where previously Abraham's steward had bowed down in prayer and thanksgiving, several shepherds and their flocks were grouped by the side of a well, the mouth of which was covered by a great stone. A stranger approached.

My brethren, whence be ye? And they said, Of Haran are we. And he said unto them, Know ye Laban the son of Nahor? And they said, We know him. And he said unto them, Is he well? And they said, He is well: and, behold, Rachel his daughter cometh with the sheep....

And while he yet spake with them, Rachel came with her father's sheep: for she kept them. And it came to pass, when Jacob saw Rachel the daughter of Laban his mother's brother, and the sheep of Laban his mother's brother, that Jacob went near, and rolled the stone from the well's mouth, and watered the flock of Laban his mother's brother. And Jacob kissed Rachel, and lifted up his voice, and wept.

Such, then, was the meeting of Jacob with his beautiful cousin after his long and difficult journey. Exiled from the tents of his father, Isaac, weary in heart, a wanderer, Jacob probably felt his cousin to be some lovely apparition, heralding the end of his harsh travel.

> And it came to pass, when Laban heard the tidings of Jacob his sister's son, that he ran to meet him, and embraced him, and kissed him, and brought him to his house. And he told Laban all these things. And Laban said to him, Surely thou art my bone and my flesh. And he abode with him the space of a month.

Two daughters were in the house of Laban: Leah, the elder, and the younger Rachel. The Old Testament describes them thus: "Leah was tender eyed; but Rachel was beautiful and well favored." That Leah was rather less striking than her sister is evident from the text, and this difference was to have some consequence in relation to Jacob.

For one month Jacob stayed with his uncle, probably doing him active service in return for the hospitality which he received. In his father's house, of course, he had scarce lifted a finger, being the prince of that patriarch. But in his uncle's house, life was somewhat less luxurious for Jacob; and it is to his credit that he offered his labor in recompense for good treatment. Laban, however, after a time, would not permit him to work without wages.

> And he said unto him, Because thou art my brother, shouldest thou therefore serve me for nought? Tell me what shall thy wages be?... And Jacob loved Rachel; and said, I will serve thee seven years for Rachel thy younger daughter. And Laban said, It is better that I give her to thee than to another man: abide with me. And Jacob served seven years for Rachel; and they seemed unto him but a few days, for the love he had to her.

From so great a devotion on Jacob's part, we can easily see that Rachel possessed endearing qualities by the score. And Jacob was always to love her so. Young, affectionate, pampered, she exerted a power over others by virtue of her "exceeding" loveliness. This power was not unrecognized by Leah, and it was to be the basis of some unhappiness for the elder sister. For Leah pined for Jacob, in secret and unrequited, and saw him concentrate his affections on that single stunning object throughout those seven years and beyond.

It came, finally, to pass that Jacob took both sisters as wives, as was often the custom in that time and place; but he favored Rachel always. After all, it was for *her* that he had labored seven years, for *her* that he had pledged his word, and in *her* interests that he had beseeched Laban, after his servitude was up, to provide for "his own house also." Leah knew this and was pained.

> And when the Lord saw that Leah was hated [that is, less cherished than Rachel], He gave her children, but Rachel had none.... And she [Leah] called the name of her eldest son Reuben: for she said, Surely the Lord hath looked upon my affliction; now therefore my husband will love me.

She was to speak this refrain several times, but the very repetition indicates an element of futility in her yearnings. For the magic pull of Rachel's charms—on Jacob as well as on others—was never really to diminish. Leah was the archetypical lady-in-waiting, the recipient of affection always, but never the recipient of love.

She bore a second son. "Because the Lord hath heard that I am not loved, He hath therefore given me this son also." Another year, and God granted her still another son. "Now will my husband be joined unto me, for I have borne him three sons." By the time of the birth of her fourth son, we may assume that Leah had resigned herself to her inferior place in Jacob's heart, and taken solace in the rewards of motherhood. For as the name of her first son, in Hebrew, means "child of affliction," the name of her fourth means "praise unto the Lord." Leah was pious and learned to take pleasure in the love of her God, who had bestowed upon her such fine sons.

Rachel was unlike Leah. Pampered, as we have noted, and favored above all others, Rachel was somewhat impetuous. Though she basked in the unremitting love of her husband, and was admired by all, she was jealous of the fecundity of her sister. She nagged

Jacob: "Give me children, or else I die! And Jacob's anger was kindled against Rachel: and he said, Am I in God's stead, who hath withheld children from thee?"

A reasonable reply, surely, but not an answer to placate the querulous Rachel. Leah, it seems, had grown to be the happier of these two sisters, for she complained not of envy but of frustrated affection towards Jacob, and took her happiness from her husband's joy in the birth of their sons, and, above all, from God's grace. She had come to religion—the religion not of her fathers, but of her husband—through suffering and meekness. Rachel was never meek, and until now had not known much suffering. Whereas she might well have prayed to God, she chose, rather, to berate man. And Jacob, instilled with the piety of his religion, and having seen already, in his own mother, the sorrow that comes from impatience, flew in anger, for the very first time, at his most treasured love.

But Rachel was not checked. Following Sarah's example, but with less laudable motives, she forced her husband, by increasing the number of his wives, to undergo all the miseries of a divided household. Rachel rejoiced at the birth of every child which Jacob fathered, perhaps out of vicarious desire, perhaps in order to show that she placed little value on her sister's fertility.

Only once did a sisterly reproach escape the lips of Leah. She said to Rachel, "Is it a small matter that thou hast taken my husband?" But then, year after year, Leah had seen her own affection slighted in favor of Rachel's unpredictable endearments.

Two other sons were born to Leah, and one daughter—an event of note, for this was the first female offspring of the patriarchs. Then it was "that God remembered Rachel; and God harkened to her and gave her children."

"God hath taken away my reproach," Rachel gratefully cried. "And she called his name Joseph, and said, The Lord shall add unto me another son." Had she been a prophet, she might indeed have presumed the reproach to have dissipated, for the good qualities of her son Joseph would cast beatification upon any mother.

It was after the birth of Joseph that Jacob said to Laban, "Send me away unto mine own place, and to my country. Give me my wives and children for whom I have served thee, and let me go, for thou knowest the service which I have done thee."

And Laban said unto him, I pray thee, if I have found favor in thine eyes, tarry; for I have learned by experience that the Lord hath blessed me for thy sake; and he said, Appoint me thy wages, and I will give it. And he said unto him, Thou knowest how I have served thee, and how thy cattle was with me—for it was little before I came, and now it is increased into a multitude, and the Lord hath blessed thee since my coming; now when shall I provide for mine own house also? And he said, What shall I give thee? And Jacob said, Thou shalt not give me anything.

Jacob's refusing all gifts from Laban originated in the refusal of Abraham to accept gifts from the king of Sodom, "lest he should say, I have made Abraham rich." For the patriarchs, as always, the issue of prosperity was to be in the hands of God. Jacob accepted his due, and no more. Though the house of Laban was to turn against Jacob in this matter, the fact is, he was acting out of patriarchal tradition.

The cattle of Laban grew marked—"speckled and ring-streaked," as the Bible puts it. This turn of events, combined with the envy of Laban's sons regarding Jacob, apparently forced Laban himself against Jacob. And then it was that God told Jacob, "Return unto the land of thy fathers and thy kindred, and I will be with thee." In any case, it cannot be charged to Laban's account that he was generous with Jacob. Laban himself admitted that his herds had increased under Jacob's management, and yet he did not offer the patriarch his due. Jacob had refused Laban's *gifts*, not his own rights.

So when Jacob had spoken with God, and the cattle marked, he "called Rachel and Leah to the field unto his flock." And he told them:

I see your father's countenance is not towards us as before; but the God of my fathers has been with me. And ye know that with all my power I have served your father; and your father has deceived me, and changed my wages ten times; but God suffered him not to hurt me. If he said thus, The speckled shall be thy wages, then all the cattle bare speckled; and if he said thus, The ring-streaked shall be thy hire, then all the cattle bare ring-streaked. Thus God hath taken away the cattle of your father, and given them to me.

And without a moment's hesitation, Rachel and Leah answered:

Is there yet any portion or inheritance for us in our father's house? Are we not accounted of him as strangers? for he hath sold us, and has quite devoured our money. For all the riches which God has taken from our father, that is ours and our children's. Now then, whatsoever God hath said unto thee, do.

Different as the sisters were, and pretty much at odds throughout their lives, when it came to the interests of their husband and children, they were in perfect accord. As they both knew, Laban had sold them both in exchange for Jacob's servitude, and had left them no inheritance. Thus, as it would appear that God himself had portioned off Jacob's share by marking the cattle, then that part of the herds, they reasoned, was Jacob's to take, for himself and his family. Amidst all the discord which Rachel had sown, at a moment of crisis they all came together and formed a united front.

But it was a hasty removal they made, and undoubtedly hard on the sisters, for they were leaving the only home they had ever known. They were to embark on a dangerous journey to a land strange to them. Leah may very well have taken solace in prayer, as had been her wont before; but Rachel, fearing for the outcome of such a journey, and never so imbued with the religion of Abraham as her sister, stole away her father's own idols.

The characters of these two women, as drawn in the Old Testament, are etched with a clarity and consistency that leaves them vividly in the mind of the reader: Leah, the submissive and unrequited, turning to God in her meek way, and rejoicing in the spiritual; and Rachel, the beautiful and headstrong, raging against the human condition, actively furthering her own designs. Proud, sure of her power over others, Rachel must have regarded an Invisible Being as a pale thing indeed for her needs. One can almost hear her thinking: Well now, an unseen Deity may be no help against the harshness of *this* journey; better I bear away my father's gods, so that we will be doubly protected. As once she commanded her husband to giver her children, so she bargained with the universe. Her insolence was very nearly magnificent. As things turned out, it was very nearly disastrous as well.

If Rachel supposed that her father would sit idly by after the theft of his images, she was very much mistaken. Jacob had fled "away unawares from Laban the Syrian, in that he told him not that he fled; so he fled with all that he had, and he rose up and passed over the river, and set his face toward the mount Gilead." And there, some days after the hasty flight of Jacob and his family, Laban overtook them, with sufficient followers "to do them hurt."

The number of her father's forces must have given Rachel pause, and it takes little imagination to picture her discomfiture while her father and husband were in conference. She had, perhaps, brought down death upon all their heads.

But Laban's reproaches were singularly mild:

> Wherefore didst thou flee away secretly, and steal away from me, and didst not tell me, that I might have sent thee away with mirth and with songs, with tabret and with harp: and hast not suffered me to kiss my sons and daughters? Thou hast done foolishly in so doing.

Jacob replied that he was not always so certain of his father-in-law's good will. Diplomatically, he professed himself to have been in fear of Laban's possessiveness with regard to Leah and Rachel. And, of course, he was, he told Laban, in great need of reaching his own home.

"And now, though thou wouldst needs be gone, because thou sore longedst after thy father's house, yet wherefore hast thou stolen my gods?" And Jacob answered, "With whomsoever thou findest thy gods, let him not live. Before our brethren discover what is thine, and take it to thee. For Jacob knew not that Rachel had stolen them." Had he known of Rachel's sacrilege, he would not have been so quick to put her head on the block.

However, during the period of Laban's search, which must, to Rachel, have seemed endless, the idols were not discovered. Thus Rachel breathed easier; and thus did she resolve never to tell Jacob of the theft. Had she done so, Jacob undoubtedly would have punished her, and severely, for not only had she stolen, and not only had her thievery exposed the entire family to danger, but she was guilty, too, of idolatry.

After the recriminations were done, and the search fruitless, Laban strove to part with his daughters in the noble fashion of his race. A heap of stones was raised by all who had met in anger, proving their reunion, and blessing their parting, with united labor, after which a feast was had.

"And Laban said, This heap is a witness between thee and me"—thus did he address Jacob.

> Therefore was the name of it called Gilead and Mizpah, for he said, The Lord watch between me and thee, when we are absent one from another. If thou shalt afflict my daughters, or if thou shalt take wives beside my daughters (though no man is with us), see God is witness betwixt thee and me. This heap be my witness, and this pillar be my witness, that I will not pass over this heap to thee, and thou shalt not pass over this heap and this pillar unto me for harm. The God of Abraham, and the God of Nahor, and the God of thy father judge betwixt us. And Jacob swore by the fear of his father Isaac. And Jacob offered sacrifices on the mount, and called his brethren to eat bread; and they did eat bread, and tarried all night in the mount.

The next morning, Laban arose, kissed his daughters and grandsons, blessed them, and departed, "returning unto his place."

Thus was discord soothed by a covenant of love—a covenant between two nations, two kings, and two religions. Such a reconciliation must have brought joy to Leah, and to Rachel, relief.

When Jacob returned to his homeland, disaster was again averted from his family's path by a reconciliation with Esau. However, Jacob and his family proceeded on to Shechem, where he "bought a parcel of a field," after erecting his tents, and "built there an altar," and there he remained, until commanded by God to "arise and go to Bethel."

These wanderings must have covered at least seven years. The youth of his children, and the safety of his herds, no doubt impelled Jacob to settle his residence in the first convenient spot in the land of Canaan. It appears strange that he did not pause at his father's house, but about such a visit scripture offers no account.

At Shechem Leah encountered a fiery trial in the insult offered to her daughter, and in the guilty conduct of her sons—deception wove a tangled web in that place. Thus, when Jacob, at the command of the Lord, removed to Bethel, he was thankful. But the journey was perilous, for "the terror of God was upon the cities that were round about them...." They passed on to Bethel, however, unscathed.

At Bethel, God again appeared to the patriarch and reiterated the age-old promise; in addition, he affirmed the change of Jacob's name to Israel, a name that was to descend though the ages to the present day, signifying the love, mercy, and glory of the Hebrew God.

Cheered by his renewed blessing, Jacob proceeded thence towards Mamre, where Isaac was then dwelling. But the entire cavalcade drew to a halt when Rachel fell ill. She was with child again, but the birth was a tortured one, and she died, after calling the babe Benoni, "son of my sorrow." Perhaps, in this name, we may see something of her unhappiness at having so often transgressed the religion of her husband, not to mention that of her father. The willful woman who trusted in no god, and who followed no morality but her own, died with a meekness that she had never displayed in life. But had she lived, she would no doubt have experienced even greater sorrow, in those evil days when Joseph, her favorite, was sold by his brethren.

In any event, there is both irony and retribution in the hard fact of her death. For once she had raged at Jacob, "Give me children, or else I die!" She had been given her children, at last, and with them, death. But this is a cruel judgment, and can only be interpreted within the context of the moral outrages she had committed against man and God. With her misuse of her own physical beauty, the disregard for her husband's religion, her wiles and cajolery, her sacrilege and dishonesty, her envy and idolatry—and most of all, her impatience with the universe—she was, in short, an all too human creature, putting trust in no one but herself, in nothing but her own powers. If retribution there was, then it was in the all too human agony of childbirth, from which there is no eartly recourse. Rachel both provokes our exasperation and demands our attention. For she is the first woman in the Bible to take on proportions larger than life; more than merely echoing Eve's pride, she seems to sum up in her nature an almost modern sensibility. Not profoundly evil in the manner, say, of Satan, or Jezebel, she was rather the pragmatist and manipulator. Her love for Jacob was genuine, if misused, and her affection for her sons, unquestioned. She had the charms of a minx, in which there is no sin, surely, for she brought great happiness to Jacob. It was not evil, then, but an unthinking independence, both earthly and metaphysical, that makes her so compelling a character. She had no faith that the world was ordered according to a special plan, and conceived that she would fulfill her own desires in that void, by wielding her personal power over others through her charms and her hard, practical intelligence. She wielded her power without regard for others, unfortunately, and it was only due to the piety of her husband and sister that she was able for so long to flaunt herself in the face of disaster.

The death of Leah is not recorded. We only know that she did not accompany the patriarch and his family to Egypt, and that she was buried, with Abraham, Sarah, Isaac, and Rebekah, in the cave of Machpelah.

Bilhah and Zilpah

Half sisters and handmaidens to Leah and Rachel, and concubines to Jacob—upon Rachel's insistence, and according to custom, as we have seen—the girls Bilhah and Zilpah bore heads of prominent lines. Through Zilpah, for instance, came the prophet Elijah; through Bilhah, Samson.

It was Rachel, we have noted, who forced her husband to increase the number of his wives, out of envy for Leah's fertility. Bilhah was her handmaiden, and so it was done. Leah was then obligated by custom to give her handmaiden Zilpah to Jacob; thus, we see in these two maids the embodiment of the tension between Rachel and Leah.

When Bilhah first gave birth, Rachel cried out that God had heard her entreaties and given *her* a son—much as Sarah had looked upon Ishmael as her own. When Bilhah gave birth a second time, Rachel looked upon it as *her* doing.

Leah, on the other hand, regarded Zilpah's children as blessings of God, and rejoiced for *their* sake, and his.

Bilhah and Zilpah were beloved of Jacob, and rode with their sons at the head of his caravan out of Mesopotamia. When Laban came after Jacob's caravan, it was the tents of these concubines that he first searched for his stolen images. Apparently they were more suspect than Rachel, who had, of course, hidden the idols. This gives some idea of the inferior position in which they were placed, and, once again, serves as evidence of Rachel's power over everyone. again, serves as evidence of Rachel's power over everyone.

And yet, though they were but concubines in the eyes of the world, they were to Jacob highly prized. For later, at the reconciliation of the patriarch and his brother, Esau, in Canaan, these two women were respectfully presented to Esau himself.

The lines descending from both women were wonderfully numerous, as Moses was later to recount.

As to their characters, little is said in Scripture. But we may infer that they were not only gracious in their conduct, as befitted the wives of Jacob, but were prudent as well, for they were used, after all, in a game of spite perpetrated by Rachel, and yet managed to survive and prosper.

To Bilhah, incidentally, we may perhaps attribute a rather passionate nature, as she was reputed (Gen. 35:22) to have lain with her husband's son by Leah, though in great secrecy.

In any case, these are two of the most prominent—and certainly the most circumspect—of all the handmaidens, servants, and concubines of the Bible.

Dinah

We have already referred, in the biography of Leah and Rachel, to the troubles attending Leah's offspring in the valley of Shechem. In pausing to consider Leah's daughter, Dinah, we may now focus briefly upon that time of dire events which so tried Jacob's soul.

Doubtless Dinah resembled her vivacious aunt, Rachel, more than her retiring mother, for one day—after Jacob had purchased land from Hamor, and settled his household—the young, impetuous girl set out, in the excitement of her naivete, for the city. We know that the patriarchs were of the land, and that they avoided cities; we have seen the extremes to which Abraham went in keeping Sarah from danger. Unprotected women were exposed to great perils in those lands, and yet Dinah set out alone. Never having been in a city, perhaps she wished to see the strange sights; or perhaps she had heard of some festival or other, and feared the dampening refusal of her family's permission. In any case, by her bold action we may surmise that she possessed a nature as headstrong and heedless as Rachel's—but without, alas, Rachel's innate cunning.

Dinah blithely set out, all by herself, and was no sooner in the city than she was used for a whore. Hamor's son Shechem saw her, desired her, and took her, probably by force. Her innocence was very quickly and no doubt ruthlessly disposed of.

When Jacob heard of the defilement of his daughter, he checked his anger until Hamor had his say. Hamor claimed that Shechem's soul "clove unto Dinah," and indeed it would appear that Shechem felt much contrition, as well as affection, toward the impetuous girl. But perhaps Hamor's motives for proposing a marriage between his son and Dinah were more mercenary than contrite, for Jacob was very rich. Dinah's brothers rose up in anger against such a pact, and demanded that Shechem be circumcised before any marriage with their sister should take place. Shechem agreed, and in the ritual the brothers of Dinah slew Shechem, his father, and all their household, and laid waste to the city, plundering everything and killing all. With whatever lust or love Shechem took Dinah, and whatever her feelings, the issue of their coupling was agony and slaughter, for which Jacob never forgave his sons, even when on his deathbed.

Presumably the brothers carried Dinah off from Shechem's house; in any event, we lose sight of this whimsical, misused child in a bath of gore.

Asenath

Joseph's wife is reputed to have been the child of Dinah, so we may say that not only agony came from that ill-fated daughter of Leah. As a babe, Asenath was abandoned at the border of Egypt; a priest of that land is said to have found her and taken her to his house, concealing her on account of her extraordinary loveliness. She seems always, however, to have felt alien to the teachings of Potiphar, the priest who adopted her.

Now, when Joseph was unjustly accused of rape by Potiphar's wife, and on the very brink of execution, Asenath, still a child, prevailed upon the priest to spare him. She claimed, not through the prophecy and oracle of the priest's religion, but through her own intuition, based upon her love for God, that she knew Joseph was innocent. She must have been, besides beautiful, a quite cunning child, for Potiphar was not easily swayed. Thus God spoke to Asenath: "As thou livest, because thou didst try to defend Joseph, thou shalt be the woman to bear the tribes that he is appointed to beget."

And bear Joseph's children she did, in time; and although she is scarcely mentioned again, it is safe to assume that she was ever a pious, faithful, and resourceful wife to Joseph.

Jochebed

From the time of Joseph to that of Moses, the Scriptures are silent with regard to the Israelites, both nationally and individually. We are given the important information that the children of Abraham "were fruitful and increased abundantly, and multiplied and waxed exceeding mighty, and the land was filled with them," but beyond that we may only surmise that they continued as before, a distinct people worshiping an invisible spiritual Being in the midst of idolators. They held no ordained worship, claimed no revealed ordinances, offered no appointed sacrifice, and had no high priest. As we have noted before, other nations feared the Israelites, and certainly this fear, and the attendant hostility, continued unabated.

A new pharaoh had risen in Egypt, who saw in the great numbers of the Israelites a threat to his power. So he attempted to afflict them by imposing great tasks and heavy burdens on them; still they continued to multiply. Heavier tasks were commanded of them, and they complied; yet they continued to multiply. Finally, like Nimrod before him, this pharaoh gave the fatal command that was to create one of the darkest hours in the dark Captivity of the Jews.

Every male child was to be destroyed at birth. Homes were ransacked and babes thrown into the Nile.

The family of Amram, son of Levi, already consisted of himself, his wife, Jochebed, a daughter, Miriam, and Aaron, the youngest, a mere toddler.

When Jochebed again become pregnant, it was under the onus of the pharaoh's decree. But she was a brave and enterprising woman, and faced the ordeal to come with great courage, bolstered by her own faith, and the faith of her husband and daughter. When the child was born, Jochebed managed to conceal him from the authorities for fully three months, before rumors spread that put the child's life in jeopardy. She hit upon the plan of putting the babe in a little ark, secured against leakage, and setting it adrift in the Nile. It was a desperate move in a desperate time. For who would feed the child, should the ark bear him safely upon the waters? The spirit of Amram and his brethren was no doubt broken by the cruelties of the pharaoh, and Jochebed seems to have acted alone in this seemingly futile endeavor. She could fall upon little but her faith for comfort, and upon the most mysterious prophecy for guidance. God had spoken to Amram, and to her daughter, but not to her, and it was not a time that signified much in the way of providence for the Hebrews. She trusted blindly in her God, and set the child on the river's brink.

But even in this most desperate act, Jochebed was not entirely without resources. She had hope, perhaps, that some compassionate stranger might pass by and take the child. So she set her daughter to watch over him; and should the little ark drift away, she instructed Miriam to follow along the bank, "to know what would be done with him."

In the biography of Miriam we shall review the journey of the little ark, for it was indeed borne over the river. Suffice it to say that the babe was miraculously returned to the mother, to be cared for under the auspices of the pharaoh's own daughter. The boy was not only saved the horror of slaughter, but the labors and burdens of his people as well; in addition, he was to have the influence and love of his own mother, and of his mother's religion, under the very protection of the pharaoh himself.

Thus was Moses' character formed, his principles fixed, and his religion obtained under the direct care of his own kind, though nominally he belonged to the Egyptian court. We do not know at what age Moses left his mother, but we may infer that her influence, not that of his adopted parent, made him what he was. No lessons given by pharaoh's daughter could have endowed him with that feeling of kinship with the Hebrews that caused him to rise up against the Egyptian who was smiting the Israelite. Had his early instruction been confined to the pharaoh's palace, his birth and nation would have been unknown to him, and he would have imbibed the principles of the Egyptians and would have bowed down before their idols. Only some very powerful force could have been at work counteracting the Egyptian influence, some very powerful force during the susceptible years of infancy and childhood. That influence, of nurse and mother, was Jochebed.

Even after the actual task of nursing was done—"and the child grew, and she [Jochebed] brought him unto Pharaoh's daughter"—it appears, she was probably still retained near her child, tending him even after he was called the princess's son. In any case, she had more than ample opportunity to inculcate in him the traditions of his fathers.

The faith and devotion displayed in Jochebed's character was evident throughout her life. As a girl she had more than once aided her brethren in the times of hardship,* and as a woman and mother, she reveals an extremely enterprising nature. It was to her faith and quick thinking, to her foresight and gentle intelligence, that the Hebrew religion owes its greatest prophet and lawgiver. She did not, apparently, live to see the apotheosis of Moses, but it can at least be said that his childhood belonged to this courageous woman.

---

*See the brief references to Jochebed's earlier bravery in Louis Ginzberg, *Legends of the Bible* (New York: Simon and Schuster, 1956), pp. 296-87.

Bithya

Moses' adopted mother stands with Hagar as one of the most remarkable Egyptians in the Hebrew narrative. Although there is not, unfortunately, so much information concerning Bithya, daughter of the pharaoh, as there is about Hagar, the favorite slave of Sarah, what evidence we have shows a strong-willed and devoted woman who truly loved the babe she had drawn out of the water.

To Jochebed we owe Moses' early conditioning; but to Bithya we owe his continued existence in the pharaoh's realms.

She assured Moses of power in the Egyptian court by pretending to be with child while the babe was being suckled at Jochebed's breast. She introduced him into the court, and brought him up in comfort and kindness. For her great love, and for her services, Moses' father always referred to her as Bithya, "daughter of God," though of course she had a royal Egyptian name.

Often she stood up against the pharaoh's suspicions concerning the remarkable child, and soothed the royal temper. Against her own customs, she married Caleb, and was a suitable wife for him. More than once she circumvented her father's schemes against the Hebrews, and for this, and for her place in the affections of Moses, it is said that she was allowed to enter paradise alive.

Miriam

We have seen that Jochebed set her daughter to watch over the little ark in which the baby Moses was placed. In this task, Miriam showed those sterling qualities of strength and courage and intelligence that were to mark her in later life. And in her boldness before Bithya we see the seeds, too, of a certain recklessness, which, though it secured to Jochebed her child again, and was therefore fortuitous, gave evidence of a character that would bow to no one, man or woman, pharaoh or prophet. Carried too far, her pride and ambition would smite the heavens, much to her disfavor. But in these mixed qualities the lineaments of a great heroine can be discerned, and she stands with Rachel as one of those biblical characters for whom the woman's submissive role in the social structure was not enough. She steps forth in all her imperfection, by her strength of soul, blazoning her image upon the mind of the reader. Like Rachel—probably more so—she is one of those who may be, and have been, judged; but she cannot be ignored or set aside as one whose virtues were purely domestic and whose faults were the result of woman's "weakness." Her virtues and faults are those of an assertive, many-sided human being.

Even before the birth of Moses, Miriam stands out in the Old Testament narrative. She doubtless took upon herself the care of Aaron in those troubled times, with her parents so distracted by their burdens. Ginzberg, in his *Legends of the Bible*,* shows Miriam reasoning with her father on the wisdom of divorce for the Jews under the pharaoh's cruel decree. And early on she is accorded the status of a seer or prophet, for her dreams foretold the coming of Moses. Her early concern for the plight of her people, and her youthful piety, bespeak a militant defender of the Hebrew cause, one whose spirit refused to be broken under the heavy weight of the pharaoh's laws. When told by her mother to look out for the Nile-borne babe, she agreed with alacrity and set out with courage beyond her years.

Hour after frightful hour the tiny ark floated on; and hour after patient hour the stronghearted sister walked along beside it, in the blazing sun, heedless of heat and fatigue. There are crocodiles in that river, and treacherous obstructions; thus, we may assume the

---

*See Ginzberg, p. 287.

journey to have been perilous in the extreme, and that Miriam was often drawn to the river's brink in fright and horror. For, besides the beasts and the elements, it should not be forgotten that this river contained, too, the corpses of Israel's infants: the Nile was the receptacle of humanity's inhuman deeds. And still the girl followed the ark, never once shrinking from the observance of her charge. She must also have witnessed the near-naked gangs of her own wretched people, who were set to work along that implacable river. Perhaps the strength of Miriam's later faith, outshining even the piety of her youth, may be traced to this horrendous journey, and to the hardships she endured and the sights she saw. For these impressions came in her tender youth, and were doubtless never forgotten. They steeled her nature, we may assume, and marked her as apart from the appointed station of her sisters in ancient times. She was not only outside the realm of domestic duty at this early age, but also alone in dangerous countryside, protected only by her cunning, her devotion, and her faith in her God.

Finally, the little vessel came to rest among some bulrushes, just as the sun was setting. Miriam sat down to wait. Then there was a commotion along the bank, and she was forced to observe the following events from her hiding place. An Egyptian procession approached, made up of beautifully clad women and many attendants. Miriam could tell the women were of high rank, and marveled at their trappings. Then she realized that it was the circle of Themestris, daughter of the pharaoh. Though later this princess was to be exalted by the Hebrews, and called Bithya as we have seen, poor Miriam could not expect anything but murder were the ark to be discovered among the rushes. For surely the offspring of the Jews' most relentless oppressor would not dare resist the royal decree.

As it turned out, the ark was discovered and its infant voyager brought to the princess. Struck by the babe's beauty, and not having the heart to throw it back in the Nile, she resisted the advice of her attendants and determined to adopt it. In a flash, Miriam saw her chance.

Emerging from her hiding place, and acting as a casual passerby,

Miriam strolled by the royal group. Amused, one of the attendants called Miriam over to see what the river had birthed. Thus Miriam boldly asked the princess whether she was to adopt the babe. If so, she went on breathlessly, then she knew of a Hebrew woman, a very skillful sort, who would nurse the child. The princess, reflecting that the babe was no doubt Hebrew, considered it fitting that a woman of that nation should nurse it. She sent Miriam to fetch the woman.

And fetch her she did, running back all the way. Flushed and excited, perhaps not believing her ears—or the shrewdness of her young daughter—Jochebed hurried back with Miriam to the princess. The royal daughter told her, "Take this child, nurse it, and let it want for nothing, for it is the adopted son of a Princess. Call him Moses, because he was drawn out the water."

And so it was that Miriam's intelligence and courage saved the life of the great lawgiver, and restored him to the care and early training of his own mother.

The years that ensued saw the greatest of upheaval in Egypt. That very babe grew to take the multitudes of his people out of that powerful land, and was the cause of a large army's being overthrown, of kings and nations swept away, of a vast wandering host. And in the period of the mighty Exodus, Miriam figures prominently.

She shared the holy triumph of her brother, responding with her whole heart to the song of praise bursting forth from the assembled Israelites on the shores of the Red Sea:

> And Miriam the prophetess, sister of Aaron, took a timbrel in her hand, and all the women went out after her, with timbrels, and with dances. And Miriam answered them, Sing, sing ye to the Lord, for He hath triumphed gloriously; the horse and his rider hath He thrown into the sea.

The Hebrew word used here may also be translated "poetess." And, indeed, Miriam was one of those gifted beings from whom the words of sacred song flowed with stunning spontaneity. At this moment, of course, she was transported with enthusiasm for the miracles she had witnessed, and was swept away with the zealous passion of her faith. Such gifts cannot be underestimated in any great social undertaking. For the members of the multitude must be bolstered by song, by dance, and by rejoicing, just as their souls must be hardened and tempered by faith. This was one of the most massive human migrations of all time, and Miriam, with her prophetic and poetic gifts, was one of its most revered leaders after Moses. She and Aaron received, too, the words of God, and the sister outshone the brother in her zeal. Her piety, under the influence of those eventful days, became enlivened by flowing verse and intensified by God's direct influence. Her militance in the Hebrew cause gave her almost legendary status.

After all, many another woman had been sent away to safety during this perilous upheaval. But not so Miriam, and it is certain that she would not have had it otherwise. That same girl who braved the banks of the River Nile, and watched over her brother, and clung fast to her faith when no one was about to protect her, rose to the forefront of the tremendous Exodus, as fearless as a woman as she had been steadfast as a girl. For her qualities of *spirit* Miriam was greatly loved by Moses and all who followed him.

A militant spirit in a great cause is a valuable quality, indeed, and its consequences are, on the one hand, highly beneficial for the movement's impetus and continued strength; on the other hand, however, it may also lead those who embody it to overstep their power and threaten the very cause they so utterly support. This latter is always an possibility, because a strict adherence to one's own piety may lead one to mistake onself for the thing revered. One may be led to extremes of unthinking actions because one has always acted with such wholehearted good intentions. For there is power in devotion, power in militance, power in the prophet and the poet: and with power of any sort there is always the danger of ambition and overbearing pride.

To these tendencies Miriam fell prey: "And Miriam and Aaron spake against Moses, and against the Cushite woman he had married." They questioned Moses' leadership and the faith of the woman he had taken for wife. Probably it was Miriam who instigated the affront, as she was more strong-willed than her brother and possessed of a forceful tongue to which people naturally paid heed. In her action, we see the first glimmerings of the fragmentation in leadership that was to result in excesses during Moses' sojourn on the Mount.

As we shall see in the chapter on Zipporah, Moses' wife is not an entirely satisfactory character in the Old Testament narrative. Little is said of her, and what little is said would seem to indicate a nature not completely compatible with that of Moses. Thus, if it was indeed Zipporah to whom Miriam referred—and there is some doubt on this question*—then it may be that Miriam discerned in the wife of her brother a creature to be despised because of her lack of zeal. It is ever so with militants. They cannot, and will not, abide those who do not share their passion. And some sympathy must be tendered the militant on this point, especially in perilous times: for a slackening of faith is a plague upon a great movement and dangerous to the entire company. For the very existence of the multitude depends wholly upon the strength of their faith, and those who do not share it, or who disdain it, may cast down the spirits of the faithful and lead them into doubt. Perhaps this is the danger that Miriam foresaw, and, jealous of her people's cause, she criticized when she thought criticism was due.

But in so acting she wreaked more havoc upon the movement than any foreign woman could have done, and threatened the cause in a more profound sense than Zipporah, in her presumed independence, could possibly have done. For Miriam questioned the leadership of Moses and the wisdom of his ways. In this her militance led her into a morass of conflict, for in seeking to purify the movement she succeeded only in polluting it. Rumors would spread; the very doubt she had berated in others was planted by her own excessive devotion. For she was not merely speaking in the interests of her cause; by turning on her brother, she spoke as well out of selfish motives.

She had power, and no doubt. And she was ambitious for her

---

*See Deen, p. 303.

nation—unquestionably so. But she saw in herself the absolute moral standard by which all others were to be judged. When a militant nature oversteps its bounds, this is the result: the presumption of a power that is only God's to wield.

> And the Lord heard it, and the Lord spake suddenly unto Moses, and unto Aaron, and unto Miriam, Come out ye three unto the tabernacle of the congregation; and they three came out, and the Lord came down in the pillar of the cloud, and stood in the door of the tabernacle, and called Aaron and Miriam; and they both came forth.

God spoke to them about the affront they had offered to Moses. And He defined for them the limits of their prophetic powers. He declared He would make Himself known to them in visions, and speak to them as in a dream:

> But my servant Moses is not so, who is faithful in all mine house. With him will I speak mouth to mouth, even apparently, and not in dark speeches; and the similitude of the Lord shall be behold: wherefore then were ye not afraid to speak against my servant Moses? And the anger of the Lord was kindled against them; and he departed. And the cloud departed from off the tabernacle; and, behold, Miriam was leprous, as snow; and Aaron looked upon Miriam, and, behold, she was leprous.

From this awful chastisement we may judge that arrogance and presumption are no small crimes in the Hebrew God's eyes. For in insulting Moses, Miriam had insulted God himself. Indeed, the Lord never spoke of Moses except as "my servant." And He told her that her prophetic powers were less than those of Moses; for only to Moses would He speak directly. Had Miriam's sin been but the impulse of the moment, the reproof alone would have been sufficient, but in order effectively to root out her criminal presumption, He inflicted such chastisement as would cause her to be shunned and loathed by the very people whom she had impressed with her importance. Aaron himself shrank from her, he who was no less guilty, but only less forceful.

We must not forget, however, that Miriam's contributions to the cause of her people were not slighted, either by God or man. Only her moment of overweening pride and ambition had brought her low, and though she must be cast out for her disease, the image of her courage would not so soon leave the minds of her nation. To be sure, out of admiration and love for her, Moses had not given reproof; it was God's to give, and God's only. No human, not even Moses, would have brought her to task for the insult, so great were her contributions heretofore. We see, then, that her sedition was as great as her courage, that both her faults and her virtues held men in awe, and required God to balance them.

Miriam stood stunned before Moses. She may have been struck dumb by the suddenness of the chastisement in those first moments. In any event, Aaron appealed to Moses for her sake.

"Alas, my lord," said Aaron to his brother, "I beseech thee, lay not the sin upon us, wherein we have done foolishly, and wherein we have sinned. Let her not be as one dead, of whom the flesh is half consumed as in the moment of her birth."

And Moses, without pause, without one word of reproof or indignation—which were, after all, rightfully his to feel—lifted up his voice in earnest prayer: "Heal her now, O God, I beseech thee." And God heard the prayer, and, in his mercy, answered it, to the effect that he would withdraw his hand after seven days, during which time, in obedience to the already instituted laws for lepers, she was to be shut out from the camp. And so highly was she regarded among the Israelites that they "journeyed not till she was healed."

For those days no one dared approach her; she was cut off even from employment; cast lower than the low and banished. Miriam had sinned not in deed but in word only; still, her words threatened the very foundations of the nation she had so deeply believed in. She had misused her gifts and, in the process, had harmed her people. Surrounded by friends and admirers and exalted by God to a high station among her countrymen, she strove in her passion to advance still higher, and fell into humiliation and sorrow.

But sorrow is often the lot of prophets and gifted ones in the Old Testament. Elijah, too, was to be sent wandering the wilderness and know great privation. And so it was with Elisha. Prophets must, it would appear, sink to the lowest level in order to rise. Defeat must temper their souls, so that patience may be taught them. The whole sense of *self* must undergo a complete transformation, in order that the divine gifts may not be used for personal ends. So it was with Miriam. Leprous, in pain and deprivation, mortified, she went into the desert, there to reflect upon the vanity of her ambition. And—more important still—she was to learn to conquer herself.

In religion as well as literature, in morality as well as philosophy, the hard-won knowledge of the self is the central issue. Passion in and of itself is not a despicable thing; far from it. It is the manner of its *modulation* and *direction* which is important. And what Miriam learned about was the limitation of militance, earthly and divine limitation. A passionate devotion must strengthen others, not undermine them; a prophetic gift must be used in the context of the greatest good, not in the furtherance of an expanding pride. And Miriam learned these things in her wandering, and returned to take again her high station among her people, strengthened, not weakened, by her chastisement.

The Israelites broke camp and pushed on. They, too, had been strengthened by Miriam's ordeal, for they were shown not only the negativity attending pride and ambition, but the truly great effort it takes to overcome such feelings. Miriam had been more than equal to the task.

Her death is recorded as having taken place at Paran, somewhat later. Her funeral was celebrated in the most solemn manner for thirty days, and throughout ancient times her tomb was an object of veneration among her people.

Miriam left us no prophetic writings; she left us only the example of her life. And in that example is all the complexity of a truly great personage. She had passion, pride, strength, eloquence, arrogance, militance, and devotion. Legends clustered about her character because her nature was resonant with conflict, and yet capable of righting itself. Her relationship with Moses lends her great glory, it is true; but on her own merits alone she stands as a fully rounded and complete human being, one whose virtues could spring from her faults, one whose faults were seen in view of her virtues and forgiven both by God and by her people. One touching legend has it, for instance, that no matter where she wandered in her banishment and disease a spring of water opened at her heels, for she has ever been associated with water, with the Nile, and with the steadfast devotion and lightning resourcefulness of her early days.*

Whether, then, Miriam was in the administration of Moses, or in exile in the desert, whether she was in high position or low, the words of the Hebrew God himself affirm the constant veneration in which this woman was held: "For I sent before you Moses and Aaron and Miriam."

Zipporah

Zipporah, wife of Moses, is scantily treated of in the Old Testament. What little we do know of her character is troubling, for she was, after all, the partner of the Israelites' great leader and lawgiver.

When Moses fled Egypt, he came to the land of the Midianites, where he encountered Jethro's daughters at a well. Moses defied the other shepherds who were gathered there by allowing the daughters' sheep to drink. For his assistance, he was taken to Jethro's house and given hospitality. From these simple occurrences, Moses' marriage sprang, for he settled his affections on one daughter, Zipporah, and took her for his wife. By her he had two sons. And with her, and their offspring, he set out, rod in hand, for Egypt again. There is no record of wooing or connubial happiness. They met; they married; they bore children.

On his journey back, Moses fell ill. The cause was mysterious, but

---

*See Stowe, pp. 93-94.

we may surmise that he had met fearful resistance from his wife on the subject of the circumcision of their sons, a custom to which the Midianites did not adhere. Only when Moses became frightfully ill did Zipporah seize upon a piece of flint and execute the ritual herself, probably on the second son. Moses then recovered. Odd as the story is in its uneven narrative, it is clear, at any rate, that Moses and Zipporah were not exactly of one mind.

Zipporah appears only sketchily again, and is not mentioned in relation to Moses' greatest days. We do hear Miriam berating Moses for his "Cushite" wife, but it is not certain whether Zipporah is meant. She is peculiarly distant from her husband's concerns throughout; and that distance may well indicate a woman who followed her own mind in questions of religion despite the tremendous influence of Moses himself.

—Women of the Tabernacle—

It is wise, in this history of the women of the Old Testament, to halt briefly and consider some of those nameless heroines who helped make such a splendid pageant out of Jewish Scripture.

Those who aided in the holy work of Moses' tabernacle are among these. For a proclamation had been made that every man and woman who had a willing heart should bring an offering to the Lord:

> And they came, both men and women, as many who were willing-hearted, and brought bracelets, and earrings, and rings, and tablets of gold.... And all the women who were wise-hearted did spin with their hands and brought that which they had spun, both of blue, and of purple, and of scarlet, and of fine linen. And all the women whose hearts stirred them up in wisdom, spun goats' hair. The children of Israel brought a

willing offering unto the Lord, every man and woman, whose heart made them willing. ... They spake unto Moses, saying, The people bring much more than enough for the service of the work, which the Lord commanded to make. And Moses gave commandment, and they caused it to be proclaimed throughout the camp, saying, Let neither man nor woman make any more work for the offering of the sanctuary. And the people were restrained from bringing.

We see, then, that notwithstanding the seditions and murmurings, the rebellions and discontents, of this multitude, there were still many whose spirits were so moved that they brought more than was necessary for the furnishing of the tabernacle. In the midst of their falling away, the people were sufficiently strong in their faith to sacrifice their possessions and lend their skills. Women threw themelves into the task, and were exalted in Scripture for their heart and for their great wisdom. The question, after all, had often been as to why Moses had brought them out of Egypt. It took wisdom, indeed, to overcome the fear and hardship of the Exodus, and the example of these women of the tabernacle points up the backbone of strength that ran through the great movement.

Their example also points up the particularly elevated position in which women were held on the journey out of Egypt. Not only was a woman, Miriam, one of the leaders, but women in general were highly esteemed for the wisdom and spirit which they contributed.

Elisheba

A much favored woman of the tabernacle was Elisheba, wife of Aaron; sister-in-law of Moses, mother of the priest Eleazar, grandmother to the general Phinehas, and sister to Nahshon. She stands second only to Miriam in the high regard in which women were held, and was one of the most indefatigable of workers and supporters, impressing all with her devotion in the work of the tabernacle. But unlike Miriam, she was to know searing agony not through her own pride but through the pride of others.

It may occasion little wonder that such an exalted woman should have as two of her sons Nadab and Abihu, who thought rather highly of themselves. For pride in lineage would be understandable in their case; however, such pride is too easily made an excuse for arrogance and criminal presumption. Having a renowned mother and father, being nephews of Moses and brothers to a high priest, they lacked the devoted character of their family. They considered no women good enough to be their wives; and when Moses himself turned from the burning bush at Sinai, they basked complacently in its light; indeed, in their pride they belittled the efforts of others and cast shadows everywhere. The great dedication of their mother was a reason for conceit to them, and they disdained all other females; as sons of Aaron, they patronized men.

Thus it was that on Elisheba's happiest day—the day of the dedication of the tabernacle—her two arrogant sons approached the portals, censers in hand, and were struck dead by God, with shafts of fire, before the very eyes of their mother.

For Elisheba this was a harsh and, no doubt, crippling event. But she stayed true to her God and as dedicated as ever to the tabernacle and its works. She may have concluded, as did her people, that there was justice in the act; for the tabernacle itself was the symbol of equality before the Hebrew God.

Puah

One of the most valuable of God's servants during the Captivity and Exodus, and therefore worthy of mention here, was the midwife. A huge nation removing itself from bondage was in great need of the ministrations of such a woman, and in the character of Puah the Old Testament pays homage to the class and profession of midwifery.

Puah was instructed by the Egyptian authorities to kill the sons of Jewish mothers when performing her duties. Puah courageously violated the mandate, this slaughter by fiat, and determined to save as many as she could of "the men children." She was also of inestimable help with the many difficult births during the march out of Egypt.

For her courage and steadfast clinging to the cause, Puah saw the babes of the Israelites grow stronger than before, and blessed by God for her sake. It is also recorded (Exod. 1:21) that midwives, like Puah, who feared God were made matriarchs of their households.

Shelomith

After the removal of his people from bondage, Moses proclaimed: "He that blasphemeth the name of the Lord, he shall surely be put to death, and all the congregation shall certainly stone him: as well the stranger, as he that is born in the land, when he blasphemeth the name of the Lord, shall be put to death."

An argument broke out one day in the Israelite camp. The son of Shelomith by a mixed marriage to an Egyptian blasphemed the name of the Lord and was accordingly stoned to death.

Tradition has it that Shelomith was a lovely and virtuous woman, with whom an Egyptian overseer, during the Captivity, fell in love; and that this overseer invaded the house of Shelomith's husband and took her. Shelomith was put out of the household when her husband discovered the transgression, and he came upon the overseer and struck him. Moses then happened by, took the part of the Israelite, and killed the Egyptian. Later, the brothers of Shelomith besought Moses to intervene with the woman's husband on her behalf, as she was blameless. Moses did so, but the husband ominously asked him whether he would kill him, too, as yesterday he had killed the Egyptian. Thus Moses fled Egypt for the Midianite lands.

Shelomith therefore represents the tragic case of a woman caught between two nations and two laws.

Achsah

After the time of Moses, and then of Joshua, came a time of many wars for the Israelites. In one of these wars, against the idolatrous city of Debir, figured the house of Caleb and his daughter Achsah.

Caleb was a prince of the tribe of Judah, so high in favor with God as to be joined with Joshua in being permitted to enter the promised land. The Lord called him "my servant Caleb, who hath followed me fully." Like Joshua, Caleb seems to have been a prince and warrior of high repute, fearless, and faithful to his God. His daughter (though not an only child) shared the consideration given her father. She was a marvelously lovely girl, and Caleb must have seen the high respect and admiration in which she was held. He conceived of offering her as a prize for the taking of Debir: "And Caleb said, He that smiteth Debir, and taketh it, to him will I give Achsah my daughter to wife. And Othniel, the son of Keaz, Caleb's younger brother, took it: and he gave him Achsah his daughter to wife."

Achsah, by her later actions, evidently concurred in this offer of her father's; indeed, her behavior upon Othniel's victory would indicate a high degree of independence, both psychologically and economically, in the station of Hebrew women. For just as Leah and Rachel had demanded of Laban their rightful inheritance, so did Achsah, with a more composed demeanor, lay claim to hers.

She must, to begin with, have been a striking woman in more ways than one. For the city of Debir was much feared, and it was an extraordinary prize indeed to provoke the storming of it. The beauty of form alone could not have unsettled Othniel to the point of undertaking such a campaign. The offer was one that had the force of a general appeal, and was flung before all the Hebrews: thus, her qualities must have transcended the physical and been considered sufficient to incite all the young men.

And it was not the promise of material wealth, either, that moved Othniel, as is proved by Achsah's actions after the young warrior's victory. For it was Achsah herself who "moved him [Othniel] to ask of her father a field or piece of land." The desire for inheritance came from her and not her husband, who seemed to have been perfectly content with the recompense of the woman herself.

In any case, Othniel complied with his young wife's request, and the land was granted. Then Achsah, continuing to show the independence of both her mind and station, went herself to her father.

> And it came to pass, as she came unto him, ... [that] she lighted off the ass; and Caleb said unto her, What wouldst thou? and she said unto him, Give me a blessing; for thou hast given me a south land; give me also springs of water. And Caleb gave her also the upper springs, and the nether springs.

In land as barren as that of Judea, land without springs was valueless; thus, Achsah had every right to request this additional gift. The affection existing between father and daughter is evident in this passage, and especially affecting. For Achsah respected her father so much that she would not speak to him while sitting upon the ass, but would alight and address him as befitted his degree and reputation. Yet neither was she meek; she did not cavil to make demand of her father, and had every expectation that her demand would be met. Caleb's immediate reply proves how justified her expectations were, and how much respect the father, in his turn, had for the daughter.

We see, too, in this woman's behavior the evidence of woman's economic station under Hebrew law. She had the right to possess landed property in her own stead, exclusive of the rights of her husband and brothers. For Caleb waited until Achsah claimed her inheritance for herself, and granted it to her alone.

Deborah

The promised land had been won, but wars continued between Israel and its neighbors. The false gods of these neighbors continued to act as "snares" for the Israelites, however, and many did "evil in the sight of God." It was a time of chaos and bloodshed, of intermittent bondage and sporadic victories for the Jews. During the time of Othniel, husband of Achsah, some manner of obedience and peace was maintained, but afterwards many of the nation fell into rebellion and idolatry again.

Many, but not all. The Old Testament speaks of "seven thousands who had not bowed the knee to Baal"; and Moses' statutes were still strongly enough in effect to be invoked repeatedly against wrong-doers. And among these few law-abiding Israelites was a truly remarkable and magnificent woman who combined in herself the offices of prophet, judge, poet, singer, and warrior, and whose intellectual and spiritual attributes fitted her well for guiding and enforcing the laws of God.

> And Deborah, a prophetess, the wife of Lapidoth, she judged Israel at that time. And she dwelt between Ramah and Bethel, in Mount Ephraim; and the children of Israel came unto her for judgment.

Deborah's greatness consisted, then, not in rank, physical beauty, or in domestic devotion, but in her superior mental and spiritual attainments, which were recognized and revered by her nation, men and women alike.

Now, the office of judge in Israel was not an hereditary one; it devolved only on those gifted to perform such services, regardless of sex or station. Often we have found, in these biographical sketches, that the women with whom we have dealt drew splendor from their husbands, though, to be sure, they deserved our attention in their own right. Sarah was a great lady apart from the greatness of Abraham, but it was as his wife that she was revered. Rebekah is almost always coupled in the mind with Isaac, even though she possessed many fine qualities of her own. And Emtelai, Leah, Asenath, and Nochebed were overshadowed by the men with whom they were connected.

We have sought, in this work, to bring all these women a little more into the light, so as to reflect upon and emphasize their various characteristics. But with certain of the women in our gallery, no emphasis is needed. Jacob was an "upright" man, and more, but it is his crafty wife who most fascinates us, with her complicated tendencies, both good and bad. Hagar, too, commands the stage when she is on it. And Miriam's nature is so dominant that even Moses seems a bit shy in her presence. As we move along, we shall encounter more such women, so that it shall not be said of the Scriptures that only "meek" females abound. What is so often meant by "meek" is actually the attitude of wife and mother. The domestic place of women in the ancient world, as we have seen in the tales of Sarah and Rebekah, was a part of the prevalent economic order. We have, it is to be hoped, brought out the valuable qualities attendant upon domestic duty, and have shown that women in Hebrew society were by no means confined to that position. Even as "meek" a character as Sarah could rise up to assert her claims; and Rebekah's domestic placidity was riven with contradiction. In Rachel, Hagar, and Miriam, of course, we see not wives and mothers primarily, but independent creatures whose wills stretched far beyond the domestic sphere. And Deborah, too, was one of these. Indeed, that she was "the wife of Lapidoth" is mentioned almost in parentheses, as secondary to her main function as prophet and judge.

It is evident, then, that in the Hebrew moral scheme God himself was no respecter of sex. He appointed Deborah as the servant of His will in a time of great trouble, when perfect hearts did not abound, and when His chosen ones were in disarray, just as He had once chosen Abraham and Jacob and Joseph. She was wife and mother, to be certain; but, like all the domestic females of the Bible, she was more than that. Indeed, Deborah was a good deal more than that.

But her domestic position was the basis upon which her divine faculties were founded, just as the fortitude and strength of the patriarchs were based upon their kinship with the land. A woman of that time who had not proved herself in homely devotion would not have commanded the basic respect of the Israelites, just as no debased merchant of the city could have commanded that agrarian people as did the farmer Abraham. An idle woman of the town could not have been a prophetess to the Hebrew nation, for they would have considered her words but mad babble. And as judge, Deborah drew upon her experience with the natural order of the Hebrew economy, in field and household, as the standard of conduct most applicable to her people, and built her wisdom upon the firm ground of woman's natural station in the Hebrew society of that day.

To Deborah's credit, it might also be pointed out that when she attained her high position as judge of the nation, she did not surround herself with royal trappings or pretentious splendor, as was the case with the Egyptian and Canaanite rulers. Her symbol was the palm tree, beneath which she sat in a serene attitude, available to all and sundry. She prophesied the dire events of the time and enjoined others to turn from their idolatry. Hers was the message of faith in a faithless day, and though a personage of simplicity and composure, she was capable, it is evident, of rising also to fiery injunction. Her nature was neither arrogant nor distant, and one had to pass through no gilded portals nor forbidding guards to reach her; the passage into Deborah's presence was purely a moral one. And that passage, for some, in so horrific a time, was more difficult, we may be sure, than gaining entry into the tombs of the pharaohs. For these idolators and murderers would be judged by Deborah according to the law of Moses, in straightforward, simple terms; and her direct simplicity was more to be feared than all the dark thunderings of the priests of Baal.

Obviously Deborah was intelligent. She had studied and absorbed the laws of her fathers, and applied them with a deep understanding of the Hebrew nation. She knew that man-made idols would scarcely suffice a *man*, for he but worshiped what he had himself made—he but worshiped himself, in fact, and there was no good in that. Moreover, she knew that through the embracing of idols the very suzerainty of the Jewish nation was imperiled in Canaan—it was she was designated idols as snares and traps for the Israelites—because the whole social fabric upon which the Jews built their power was dependent upon a religious and political unity, so that resistance could be shown those jealous nations who used their gods as bait for the unwary. If that resistance could be weakened—when the unwary snatched at the bait—oppression and disintegration would be certain to follow.

As a woman she had particular insight into the threat of idolatry. For she enjoyed, with other Hebrew women, the rights of law, which were unknown in other nations. When Jael, an idolatress, came to her for help because Jael's daughter had been ravished by the Canaanites, Deborah informed her in no uncertain terms of the connection between idols and woman's oppression, and foretold like treatment for many other women should idolatry continue. Like Miriam, Deborah was truly militant in the political cause of their religious purity, for the two went hand in hand. Unlike Miriam, however, she did not place herself before the cause, and she always based her actions on the law.

Jabin, the Canaanite king, and his general Sisera were at that time wreaking havoc on the Hebrew nation. The wisdom of Deborah was called upon to obstruct them. And here, as always, her courage and understanding came to the fore, as well as her militant strength in support of her people.

And she sent and called Barak the son of Abinoam out of Kedesh Naphtali, and said unto him, Hath not the Lord God of Israel commanded, saying, Go and draw toward Mount Tabor, and take with thee ten thousand men of the children of Naphtali and the children of Zebulon? And I will draw unto thee Sisera, the captain of Jabin's army, and his chariots and his multitudes; and I will deliver him into thine hand. And Barak said unto her, If thou wilt go with me, then I will go; but if thou wilt not go with me, then will I not go. And she said, I will surely go with thee; notwithstanding the journey shall not be for thine honor; for the Lord will sell Sisera into the hand of a woman.

It would appear that, like many of his fellows, Barak was wanting in the faith which Deborah had. She was exhorting him in the name of God and the Hebrew people; yet still he clung to his fears, and would not undertake the campaign unless the prophetess herself should accompany him. This request of Barak's indicates the high repute in which Deborah was held; but it also indicates that even as courageous a man as Barak was in need of idols—in this instance, Deborah herself. Thus, to bring this failing home to him, she tells him that not to him shall fall the glory of the campaign. *He* would put conditions on his obedience to God; Deborah obeyed *her* God without reservation. In short, Barak believed in Deborah, whereas Deborah knew such belief to be misplaced.

The judge of the nation rose and went with Barak, first to collect the necessary troops from Zebulon and Naphtali, and then to Mount Tabor, where Sisera and his tremendous army marched to meet them. The raising of ten thousand in such dark times was a feat of some magnitude. But Deborah's tongue was fluent and her passion contagious, and Israel was fired with her call to arms. Later, her gift of poetic expression was to be superbly exercised, upon the foretold victory, but even in the raising of the army we may assume that her poetic faculties were utilized, and that she inspired by the intensity and beauty of her faith.

Still, Sisera's army constituted a mighty foe, with its iron chariots and well-trained infantry. Thus, Barak's timidity was not his alone; though bolstered by Deborah's exhortations, and by her fearless example, still the Israelites required solace, and Deborah told them not to be "faint of heart," for of what good would their households be, and of what benefit their lands, should an idolatrous horde sweep Israel away and defile the laws that had ordered those households and secured those lands.

Deborah was speaking not only on behalf of her God but in defense of a way of life. For the Mosaic law forbade such things as the alienation of property and the mistreatment of the old, the infirm, and the afflicted; there were strictures on excessive wealth and provision for the poor. The whole egalitarian structure of Jewish life was in danger of giving way to nations whose laws condoned the excessive accumulation of property and wealth and the casting out of the poor, and whose treatment of the aged and unfortunate was brutal. And women, to the Canaanites, were but objects, to be used, soiled, and disowned. Deborah knew well the fate of her and her sisters should the Canaanites triumph; but she was "strong of heart" and steeled by her faith in God and the Hebrew law.

So it was that the Israelites were called by Deborah to rise up: "Up! for this is the day in which the Lord hath delivered Sisera into thine hand: is not the Lord gone out before thee? So Barak went down from Mount Tabor, and ten thousand men after them."

It was an utter rout of the Canaanite army. The fierceness of the battle was extreme, but the courage and fortitude of the Israelites, ill-trained though they were, won the day, and only Sisera himself escaped death on the battlefield. He fled into the hills, and there came upon Jael's tent—Jael, whose daughter he had taken part in raping. Not knowing the mother, he sought refuge in her tent. She granted it. And there she killed him. Barak had indeed been robbed of complete victory by a woman's hand. But he had been denied the honor of the victory as well. That "the hand of the children of Israel prospered and prevailed against Jabin, King of Canaan," was due, in complete measure, to the inspiration and dedication of the prophetess Deborah.

In addition to the legacy of her courage, prophecy, sound intellect, and unwavering faith, Deborah left us with one of the finest pieces of poetry ever composed, which she sang on the day of victory for her people. It shows how closely she rivals the Psalmist of the Bible and the other prophets in their most transported moments. In this song, we find Deborah eschewing all glory for herself, and calling upon the people to join with her in "blessing the Lord for the avenging of Israel." She goes on to say that before him "the earth trembled, and the heavens dropped, and the clouds spilt water." "And the mountains shook, even Sinai, before the Lord God of Israel," she says, thus illustrating the power, not of man, but of the God who inspires him. Then she describes the situation of her people before she rose to judge among them: they were compelled to travel in bypaths, since the main roads were commanded by their enemies; the towns and farms were decimated, or unprotected; and the people were continually exposed to danger.

In these verses she calls herself neither judge, nor prophetess, nor princess, but mother, thus showing her wisdom in laying the firm foundation of the Hebrew familial order beneath her poetic flights. And she meant, of course, that she was mother to a whole people, and that she had been vouchsafed the role of judge, judge and prophet, among them. She asks nothing more than that she should be remembered thus.

She continues on to bless those who had joined in the call to arms, from lords down to water-carriers. She blesses them for their courage and for their refusal to bow down before idols and forsake the old laws. She bids all classes and conditions to speak, and to thank God for their preservation.

When, next, she draws attention to herself, and proclaims that "The Lord made me have dominion over the mighty," she is speaking as the mother and judge of her nation, and thus *for* her nation. Gathered in her being was all the dormant righteousness and strength of the Hebrew people, and in giving her victory, God returned to the Jews their promise and rights.

Vividly she describes the downfall of the enemy and the death of Sisera; she even imagines his waiting mother, a mother much different from the Israelite. For this mother wonders, "Why is his chariot of iron so long in coming, why do the wheels tarry? Have they not sped? have they not divided the prey: to every man a damsel or two; to Sisera a prey of many colors, a prey of many colors of needlework, meet for the necks of them that take the spoil?"—and thereby the poetess points up the degraded position of women outside the Mosaic law, who look with approval upon the rape and pillage of another people. There is satire here, and more: for the Israelite, according to Mosaic law, was not to look upon his neighbor or upon other nations as prey, but as brothers; and thus the dire act of Jael in killing Sisera is juxtaposed as a king of retribution against those who use force instead of love. Jael, indeed, was avenging a love that was sullied and crushed, the love and youth of her own daughter, ravished by the Canaanites. Thus, again, we see Deborah drawing upon her deep knowledge of Hebrew law, and bringing it to poetic expression in the horrendous account of the bloody war.

But the most beautiful verse is the last, in which the prophetess Deborah likens faith to the sun, and it may serve as a fitting tribute to this most remarkable woman:

> So let thy enemies perish, Jehovah!
> But thy people shine out as the sun in his might,
> When he riseth and spreadeth his banner in heaven,
> And Israel's children rejoice in the light!

Jephthah's Daughter

A century or more after Deborah's great victory, the Israelites were again plunged into idolatry and foreign oppression. Out of the darkness of this time, the figures of a father, Jephthah, the ninth of Israel's judges, and his only child, a daughter, emerged as the agents of Providence. And this daughter was willing to give up her life for her God.

Jephthah was "a man of valor," and a man of great physical strength besides. He was the illegitimate son of Gilead, a prominent Hebrew, by a foreign harlot. Despite the slur of his birth, as some of his brethren saw it, and despite the very idolatry of those same hypocritical brethren, Jephthah rose to become a great general in the cause of the "one sole invisible God."

Banished from his father's house for the reason of his shady birth, Jephthah fell in with a band of outcast desert marauders, who pillaged the countryside and lived in rude and primitive ways. Jephthah became their leader after a time, and was subsequently feared throughout the nation. Though he took women for spoil, in the manner of such men, he does seem to have married; and he fathered a daughter, whom he cherished.

Between the Gileadites and the Ammonites a war then broke out; and because Jephthah was feared universally for his military cunning, and for his ferocity, he was asked by his father's people to command the Gileadite army. Jephthah was understandably wary, and demanded the ratification of all agreements between himself and his brethren, after which he settled temporarily at Mizpah, where he installed his daughter and their household. At first he tried to work out a reconciliation with the Ammonites; that having failed, he was moved by "the spirit of the Lord" to scour the countryside, as Deborah had before him, so as to raise an army.

Again, as in Deborah's time, the idolatrous enemy was numerically and militarily superior. And Jepthah lacked Deborah's unwavering faith. Whereas Deborah had exhorted her troops in the name of God and the Hebrew nation, Jephthah committed himself to a reckless vow to God, in order to raise his own and his troops' spirits:

> If thou shalt without fail deliver the children of Ammon into mine hands, then shall it be, that whatsoever cometh forth of the doors of my house to meet me, when I return in peace from the children of Ammon, shall surely be the Lord's, and I will offer it up for a burnt offering.

Now, there are two ways of looking at this vow. We know from Moses' law that human sacrifices were forbidden; therefore, should some commentators be correct,* then Jephthah was simply offering one of his household to labor his life in the service of the tabernacle, where nonhuman burnt offerings were made. But it may be, also, that at this dark time, Moses' law was not entirely or strictly observed, as the Gileadites themselves were riven with idolators, and fought for Israel only because they considered it preferable to Ammon. Many, it would seem, were mercenaries; and Jephthah himself, though inspired by God, evidently had not the intellect or consistent devotion of Deborah, or else he would not have made the vow in the first place. To insure victory, he may indeed have been offering one of his household as a human sacrifice.

But in either case, the devotion of the daughter, as we shall see, was magnificent.

As it happened, under God's guidance, Jephthah's army decimated the Ammonites, and most of their cities fell.

Jephthah rushed back to Mizpah, glowing with victory. Doubtless he expected a servant to greet him at the door, before his daughter, as would have been the custom. But the young daughter herself doted on the man. She had seen him rise from a crude desert condition to reclaim his birthright and, by his victory, become the first man in the whole nation of Israel. So she commanded her household to step aside, and placed herself at the door, so as to be the first to greet her father in his triumph.

---

*See Deen, p. 75.

Glory died in Jephthah's heart when he saw her rushing to him. "Alas, my daughter!" he cried, "thou has brought me very low, and thou art one of them that trouble me: for I have opened my mouth unto the Lord, and I cannot go back."

To which the daughter bravely answered, "My father, if thou hast opened thy mouth unto the Lord, do to me according to that which hath proceeded out of thy mouth; forasmuch as the Lord hath taken vengeance for thee of thine enemies, even of the children of Ammon."

However, requiring strength to face her ordeal, the daughter requested of her father a period of two months, so that she might go wandering the mountains and "bewail her virginity." From this statement, we may assume that she was simply to be placed in the service of the tabernacle, where a life of celibacy was requisite. But certainly a young girl who had had every expectation of making a good marriage and of bearing children, of knowing human love and physical passion, might well choose to bewail the fact that she would never know such pleasures, because she was to be cut off in her first bloom and destroyed.

In any event, the daughter obediently returned to her father, and he "did with her according to his vow." Whether we take the story at face value, and conclude that Jephthah did, in fact, burn his daughter alive, or whether she entered into the service of the tabernacle, the fact remains that Jephthah's only daughter has come down to us as a symbol of selfless sacrifice.

Job's Wife

When Job, one of the wealthiest men of his time, was struck down and tried by the Lord, and lost his cattle, flocks, camels, and all his children, and was blighted, moreover, by leprosy, his wife uttered a wrenching cry for which even today we may not damn her. We might only shake our heads over it. She told him, as he sat on the ash heap outside the city walls. "Do thou still retain thine integrity? Curse God, and die!" Quick death was supposed to follow upon such a curse, and Job's wife preferred that such an instant demise should visit her husband, than that he should die so horribly and so slowly. But even in his extremity, Job would not take the name of his God in vain.

Bewildered and stunned by calamity, Job's wife was not wicked that her faith wavered so; her advice came from her despairing heart, and out of her deep sorrow for the man. Her faith was not so strong as his, and she turned from him in the most vile depths of his disease. But Job himself did not resent her for her actions, and later, upon his miraculous restoration, had several sons by her.

"Curse God, and die!" This woman's cry, drenched with despair, stands yet as one of the most terrifying and heart-rending statements uttered.

Tamar

The example of Tamar, daughter-in-law of Judah, illustrates a marriage law of the time which women were able to utilize for their own protection.

The law, instigated by Moses, required the marriage between a man and his brother's widow if there were no male issue from the first marriage.

Tamar was wife to two of Judah's brothers, one after the other. These brothers pursued, evidently, each his own evil path, for they were "slain by the Lord." Still, Judah promised Tamar his own son, when the boy came of age, as recompense for her two brief, ill-fated, and childless unions.

As it turned out, however, Judah procrastinated; he withheld his son even beyond the age of marriage. Apparently he felt Tamar to be under a curse, and possibly a luckless bane upon his family. After Judah's own wife died, Tamar rose up to assert her right to motherhood.

Her plan was a clever one, and gives some indication, too, of the beauty of her form—her name is the same as that of a tall and stately tree of Mesopotamia. She had decided to set out alone on a dangerous and desperate mission, intending not to hide but to flaunt her loveliness. In her mind, it would appear, the rights to which she was entitled by Mosaic law justified the extreme plan that she had devised.

She had heard that Judah was to meet with other governors upon the hills of Timnath, and she knew as well that there would be a festival attending the meeting. She removed, then, her widow's weeds, and dressed herself in a brilliant brocade robe. And, of course, she veiled her face. She then betook herself to Timnath, and there posed seductively by the path the governors would take into the hills.

Judah saw her and mistook her for a harlot. "Go to, I pray thee," he said to Tamar, "let me come in unto thee."

Saucily, Tamar replied: "What wilt thou give me, that thou mayest come in unto me?"

Judah said, "I will send thee a kid from the flock. And she said, Wilt thou give me a pledge, till thou send it? And he said, What pledge shall I give thee? And she said, Thy signet, and thy bracelets, and thy staff that is in thine hand. And he gave it her, and came in unto her, and she conceived by him."

Whereas Potiphar's wife, in Asenath's story, lied out of frustrated desire and selfishness, Tamar's deception was in defense of her own rights under Mosaic law. She had had, let us remember, no recourse *but* deception, as Judah had consistently, until now, ignored her.

Tamar went back to her home, with Judah's personal articles in tow. She resumed the widow's garments, and was thus attired when the kid from Judah's flocks arrived, with Judah's request that his possessions be returned to him. Tamar refused.

Months later word reached Judah that his daughter-in-law was "with child by whoredom." Rising up in anger, Judah commanded that Tamar be brought before him and burned on the spot, which was the penalty for such a crime. Tamar came to Judah, but it was only the patriarch's cheeks which burned. For she cast down before him his own signet, bracelets, and staff, and asked, "Discern, I pray thee, whose are these?"

Judah was, predictably, abashed. He admitted that Tamar "hath been more righteous than I," and proclaimed to all the people that Tamar had acted wisely, courageously, and according to the law; and he absolved her of guilt.

There is great Rabelaisian humor in this story, as well as wisdom. The Scriptures abound in tales of animal passions, and reflect not immorality but a high moral tone in the telling of such tales. The Jews have in the Old Testament a *Decameron* of their own, in which licentiousness is described within the context of moral choices. Tamar was a woman who in any other nation would have lacked the means of attaining her rights; indeed, she would have had no rights to attain. Tamar not only knew her rights, but had the law to support her, so that no man could say she had acted wrongly.

She used woman's wiles, it is true, and deceptively wanton behavior, but only because her coupling with Judah was, in fact, prescribed by law. That she had to hoodwink the man was not her fault, and if, in his mind, she was a harlot, well, that reflected on his character, not hers. She had a claim on the man's seed, and that, under law, was that. The real villain in this tale—as he himself admitted—was Judah.

Subsequently Tamar bore twins, and knew the happiness of motherhood, which she had gone to such lengths to obtain. But she suffered troubles, too, over the question of her sons' birthrights; still, through her sufferings descended David, king of kings.

Naomi and Ruth

In the barbaric period of the judges, the period which, for all its idolatry and bloodshed and oppression, witnessed the magnificence of Deborah and the inspiration of Jephthah's daughter, saw also the simple beauty of a mother and her daughter-in-law, whose story falls somewhere between the venality and valor of the period, in a gentle domestic sphere that bespeaks both the pain and the joy of the ordinary faithful Hebrew.

Forced in this terrible time from his tribe in the land of Judah—for famine raged there—a man called Elimelech took his wife, Naomi, and his two sons to a remote region known as Moab, where they settled. Distant from and fearing the painful seizures through which the nation of Israel was passing, and hoping to preserve his family from harm, Elimelech did not send his sons to their homeland for wives. Instead, the two young men married women of Moab, women foreign to the Hebrew religion. But these sons could not have chosen better wives, in any case, for Orpah and Ruth were good and loving wives, and the latter was highly regarded for her beauty.

Elimelech suddenly died, and then the sons, each leaving a bereaved woman behind. Naomi, whose nature might once have been accepting and gentle, and who in her girlhood was probably rather spritely, became the most cast down and depressed of the three widows, for she had, after all, lost both her husband and sons. Then, too, she was in a foreign land whose people did not practice her faith, and doubtless she felt horribly alone and far indeed from home and from the warmth of her own kind.

It is little wonder that she set her sights on a return journey to Israel. She had heard, too, that the famine which had struck her people down and forced her family's removal was over: "the Lord had visited His people with bread." There was, then, no reason for her to remain among alien persons and their alien gods, and she at length decided to embark upon the arduous trip back to Judah.

As to her daughters-in-law, Naomi's feelings appear to have been mixed. In her depression, too, she had become somewhat brittle, and did not believe that foreign women could feel as she did, though they were, the three of them, closely tied by tragedy, and bound, of course, by custom.

What she told Orpah and Ruth may be interpreted either as an expression of bitterness at her own lot or as an affectionate severing of the customary bonds in the girls' own interests. Or perhaps Naomi associated them with her own grief, and wished to be rid of them, to be free to go home and die. Or it may have been a mixture of all these feelings. In any case, she said to them: "Turn again, my daughters; why will ye go with me? Are there yet any more sons in my womb, that they may be your husbands? Turn again, my daughters, go your way, for I am too old to have an husband. If I should say that I have hope tonight that I should have an husband, and bear sons, would ye tarry for them till they were grown? Would ye stay from having husbands? Nay, my daughters, it grieveth me for your sake that the hand of the Lord hath gone out against me."

The sorrowing woman, bleak in her despair, probably had no thought that the girls would not, in fact, return to their mothers. And Orpah, a good woman, but not given to the religion of Abraham, reacted as the mother-in-law had expected, and "they lifted up their voices and wept again, and Orpah kissed her mother-in-law," which means that the girl accepted the proffered release from the customary obligation. But Ruth reacted in a manner very surprising to Naomi, for this daughter-in-law "clave unto her." Indeed, Naomi could not believe such devotion.

"Behold," she said to Ruth, "thy sister has returned unto her people and unto her gods; return thou after thy sister-in-law."

We see here a cruel fact of the ancient world, issuing from the mouth of this hard and embittered woman. And yet it is a fact also of modern times, that persons of one faith are not given to accepting or trusting those of another. Intolerance, indeed, may be the result of incomprehension such as Naomi shows here but it is intolerance that works against the very basis of a religion like Judaism. For Jews must never, not in times as dark as the days of the judges, nor under more recent afflictions, turn against those who would tender the hand of friendship and loyalty simply because that hand is foreign. To be chosen by God is not to be special to him, and apart or aloof from all others, but to be under obligation to him and to his laws of love and compassion. Judaism, of course, is not the only religion to have adherents such as Naomi, who would not accept the simplicity of another's devotion, when, in fact, that devotion was the essence of her own faith. The Old Testament provides us here with a striking example of the necessity for tolerance and understanding in a world of conflicting beliefs.

But, Ruth was not to be deterred. And she spoke to her mother-in-law words that are often thought to have been uttered by one lover to another, so crystalline is the affection expressed. But these famous words were simply the verbalizing of the strong feelings existing between a Moabitess and a Jewess, and consecrate a friendship that—at least on Ruth's part—went far deeper than passion or troth. And it is not by the way that Ruth's words comprise some of the most beautiful poetry in all the Bible.

Ruth said to Naomi:

> Entreat me not to leave thee, or to return from following after thee; for whither thou goest I will go, and where thou lodgest I will lodge; thy people shall be my people, and thy God my God. Where thou diest I will die, and there will I be buried: the Lord do so to me, and more also, if aught but death part thee and me.

Naomi was undone by these words, and softened her bitterness to the point of granting her daughter-in-law's desire. God had, then, sent her consolation, in her loneliness given her an earthly friend, thus not only pouring spiritual balm into the bruised and hardened heart but providing some being on whom its affections might again find rest, and whose faithful love would fill the void. To the bereaved mother, left alone in her age, a gnarled tree from whom no fruit would ever drop again, Ruth's affection must indeed have seemed, after so much adversity, too good to be true. Without Ruth, of course, Naomi would have been alone, and would probably have perished.

But Naomi was a poor woman. Her return to her homeland would secure her some provision, but she was, in any case, without husband or sons. And in so uncertain a time for her people, she might not even find the provision due her. She took her daughter-in-law by the hand, and with her cast out into a void—a long and dangerous journey to a precarious place.

As for Ruth, her feelings must have been especially fearful. She bade farewell to the scenes and associations of her youth, not for a period but for a lifetime, and went forth to a land and a people she had never known. She did so unhesitatingly, and resigned herself to her mother-in-law's fate, whatever that might be, but it would be preposterous to assume that she had no fears. She was young, she was lovely, and she was traveling with only an old woman, to whom she was both protector and helper.

Each of these women was courageous in her own way, and displayed the steadfastness and fortitude of the Bible's great female characters, though they were but ordinary and unpretentious women, driven neither by revelation nor by rectitude, but by a simple desire to go to the land of Israel.

We are not told how long they traveled, nor are we told what dangers they may have encountered, but we have only to remember the wanderings of Abraham and Sarah or of Jacob and his wives to form some idea of the fearsome circumstances.

At any rate, "it came to pass, when they were come to Bethlehem, that all the city was moved about them, and they said, Is this Naomi?" It had been years since she had been among her people, and the arduous journey had undoubtedly taken its toll, so that the once fair wife of Elimelech occasioned a great deal of comment.

The scene gives us a picture, too, of that primitive union of family and tribe peculiar to early Judaism. It was a time when men were not so engrossed with their own concerns that they felt no sympathy with those outside their own limited circle. They could spare both time and feeling to be moved at the return of a countrywoman who had been absent so long, and to grieve with her at those heavy afflictions which caused her to reply to their eager greetings, "Call me not Naomi, call me Marah, for the Almighty hath dealt very bitterly with me—I went out full, and the Lord hath brought me home again empty. Why then call ye me Naomi, seeing that the Lord hath testified against me, and the Almighty hath afflicted me?"

Now, in Hebrew, Naomi means "pleasant" and Marah means "bitterness." Thus we see Naomi cast down just as much at the end of the long journey as she had been at the beginning. And just as forgetful of her remaining blessing—Ruth.

Of course, she felt deeply the contrast between her return to, and her departure from, the Israelites. We see her shrinking from the name of her youth and embracing bitterness and sadness. But we may question the emotion expressed by Naomi. It was a form of self-laceration. No one would deny the greatness of her losses; on the other hand, she had survived them and gained that greatest of all blessings—a true friend. That she should recount her troubles to her people is understandable, as they would want to know of her every trial; but that she should dwell upon those troubles, and flagellate herself mentally because of them, is neither reasonable nor meet for a follower of Abraham and Moses and Miriam. Only because her countrymen rejoiced in seeing her and endeavored to alleviate her sorrowful lot did Naomi begin to settle into a humble calmness.

And this calmness reflects well on the generality of her countrymen. For the years of famine and war had not dealt so kindly with them, either, and yet they strained to make provision for the returning widow and her daughter-in-law. Ruth's own industry was decisive here, and Naomi did not feel an immediate need to make an appeal to her late husband's relatives. It was the time of the barley harvest, and the young Ruth was sent, willingly, into the fields.

Near the city of Bethlehem was a great mansion, surrounded by fields and groves, and this place belonged to Boaz, a prominent, pious, and wealthy Hebrew who was related to Naomi's late husband. Ruth went to work in this man's fields, purely, as the Bible says, by "hap." She did not seek out this wealthy connection, for she had not been instructed to do so by Naomi. Naomi had not told her of her relation with Boaz and simply sent the girl into the fields with her blessing. Ruth simply gravitated, like so many of the poorer Hebrew workers, to the rich man's fields. For Boaz was known to be a kind and generous man.

According to his wont, Boaz was in the fields. He was there not simply to look after his own interests—for he had no fear of mismanagement or thievery—but to tender his respect to the workers and to bless them. Also, he was a strict follower of Moses' law: "When ye reap the harvest of the land, thou shalt not wholly reap the corners of the field, neither shalt thou gather the gleanings of thy harvest; thou shalt leave them for the poor and the stranger."

Among the poor who followed the reapers was Ruth. And Boaz saw her and said, "What lovely damsel is this who followeth the reapers?" He was told of her connection to Naomi, of whose return Boaz was aware, but who, according to custom, would not seek a kinswoman unless sought.

Boaz said to Ruth: "Hearest thou, my daughter, wander not about the fields, but glean here in mine, and keep fast to my maidens. When thou art athirst ask the young men to draw for thee. I will speak to them that they treat thee well." Ruth, grateful and surprised at the notice of the master of the field, knelt at his feet and bowed her head before him, saying, "How have I found grace in thine eyes that thou shouldst thus kindly notice a stranger?"

"All thou hast done to thy mother-in-law since the death of thy husband hath been fully shown me," said Boaz, "and how thou hast left thy father and mother, and the land of thy nativity, and art come into a people thou knewest not heretofore. The Lord recompense thy work, and a full reward be given thee of the Lord God of Israel, under whose wings thou hast come to trust."

Ruth, in reply, showed both grace and gratitude: "Let me always find favor in thy sight, for thou hast comforted me and hast spoken friendly unto thy handmaid, although I be not one of thy maidens."

"Come hither at meal-time," said Boaz, "and eat of my bread, and drink of our vinegar."

At midday the reapers all assembled to dinner, accompanied by Boaz. Ruth was called, and was served by the master of the farm, who gave her parched corn, bread, and vinegar. When the master of the field departed, he gave Ruth into the care of his reapers, with a charge to leave a little for her to glean as she followed. In the evening all departed, and Ruth with them. She had beaten out her gleanings, which amounted to a bushel of barley.

When she presented this largesse before Naomi, the old woman was amazed. "Truly, thou hast been successful, my daughter! where wroughtest thou today?" Ruth told her the name of the kind man who had favored her in the fields, and Naomi, shaking her head in wonder, told her that Boaz was their kinsman. The old woman, too, had come to love Ruth for her devotion, and told the girl, "The Lord will reward thee, my child, for thy industry and thy piety."

Naomi's bitterness had indeed been softened, and she now saw in the virtuous Ruth a reward from God. For she remembered the law of Moses. In effect, when a man dies, the next of kin is obliged to marry his widow and raise up an heir for his brother's name. Boaz was the nearest living relative of Naomi's family by Elimelech, but never had she entertained the idea of his marrying the humble Moabitess. Never, that is, until now, when the man's favor had been so obviously displayed before all the people.

She told her daughter-in-law, "Our kinsman Boaz winnoweth barley tonight, on the threshing floor. Wash thyself, therefore, anoint thee, and put thy raiment upon thee and get thee down to the threshing floor; make not thyself known to him until he hath done eating and drinking; when he lieth down, mark the place, and when he is asleep, lift up the mantle which covers him and lie down at his feet under cover."

What Naomi communicated to Ruth here was one of the touching customs of the time. For to act in such a manner was a token that a woman claimed the fulfillment of the law and the protection of her kinsman.

Ruth betook herself to the threshing place, where she concealed herself. Long must she have watched Boaz at the winnowing and then at the feast. With a tired but happy heart, Boaz must have laid himself down upon straw and thrown his mantle over himself. Ruth now approached, and fearlessly, for she knew her mother-in-law understood well the customs of the land. Awakening, Boaz inquired who it was that sought his protection beneath his mantle.

"I am Ruth, thy handmaid," she replied. "Spread therefore thy skirt over me, for thou art the nearest kin to my husband."

When Boaz became aware it was the lovely and virtuous Ruth who thus sought him as a husband, his heart warmed towards her. His gratitude was great that she had preferred him, a man nearly twice her age, to the many young men who admired her.

"Blessed be thou, my daughter," said he, "for thou hast shown more judgment and kindness in thy latter end than at the beginning, as thou followedst not young men," among whom, he averred, she had gained a fine reputation for virtue. He proceeded to inform her that there was yet a kinsman still nearer than he, whose duty it was to perform the husband's part; but if he refused, even he, Boaz, pledged himself to do so, "as the Lord liveth," and bade her lie down until morning. When they awoke, he gave her six measures of barley, so that she and her mother-in-law should not want, and sent her back to Naomi. And then he set about the business.

The hope of obtaining as beautiful a girl as Ruth for his wife so provoked Boaz that he took pains to have the affair settled as quickly as possible. That day he appointed ten of the elders of Bethlehem to meet him at the city gate, when he knew Elimelech's nearer relative would be present.

Boaz went to the place, saluted the elders, and they all sat down. When the relative appeared, Boaz called him over and laid before him the intentions of Naomi to sell a piece of their late kinsman's land. As closest relative, would the man buy it? The relative agreed. As an "encumbrance," Boaz informed him, the girl called Ruth the Moabitess must he also marry and get with an heir. At this the relative balked, as he did not wish to mar his own inheritance by bringing a wife and more children in to his household. So to Boaz the kinsman said: "I give thee my right as next of kin, for I cannot redeem it."

Boaz willingly agreed to take the land and Ruth. In fulfillment of the law used on all such occasions, he plucked off his kinsman's shoe as a token that he took from him the inheritance. Then, turning towards the elders and people who were gathered there, he said: "All ye assembled here are witnesses this day, that I have bought all that was Elimelech's of the hand of Naomi; moreover, Ruth the Moabitess have I taken to be my wife, to raise up the name of the dead upon her husband's inheritance, that his name be not cut off from among his brethren, and from the gate of this city. Ye are witnesses this day!"

The elders assented, as did the people. And when all was silence, one of the elders spoke in solemn tones: "The Lord make this woman, that is come into thy house, like Rachel and Leah, which two did build the house of Israel; and do thou worthy in Ephratah, and be faithful in Bethlehem; and let thy house be like the house of Phazer of the seed which the Lord shall give thee of this young woman."

The references here to Jewish history give some idea of the strongly persisting traditions of the Israelites in this place, though the time generally was uncertain and dark. And we see, too, the great respect which was held for the law, and the necessity of all things being done in the light of day and above board. Boaz was rich and powerful enough to have cheated his kinsman of the chance to his rightful inheritance, and to have thumbed his nose at the old traditions. But instead he appeared before the elders of Bethlehem and the townspeople and appraised his kinsman of his rights, openly and respectfully, as was the law. Thus the words of the elder displayed, in addition to the pious references, the very spirit of the Hebrew traditions, and conveyed the desire that Boaz follow in those traditions.

And so he did: for as the great-grandfather of David, the name of Boaz must indeed be famous in Judah and dear to Israel. The trust that grew out of bitterness in the heart of Naomi, and the filial obedience and unswerving devotion of Ruth, were both rewarded, for in due course Ruth became Boaz's wife and bore him a child.

Naomi, who had believed herself a gnarled and withered tree, a fruitless old woman, "took the child, and laid it on her bosom, and became nurse to it." The women of Bethlehem told Naomi, "Blessed be the Lord, who hath not left thee this day without a kinsman, that his name may be famous in Israel. And he shall be unto thee a restorer of life, and a nourisher of thine old age, for thy daughter-in-law who loveth thee, and who is better to thee than seven sons, hath borne him."

The babe was indeed a restorer of Naomi's life; moreover, the bond between Naomi and her daughter-in-law was now universally recognized. Ruth was perceived as being better than "seven sons" (in the Hebrew the number seven signifies an unlimited number) and she was held up, therefore, as a mother fit to bear sons for Israel.

Now, an objection is sometimes made: should Ruth, a foreign woman, have been the ancestress of David, the elected servant of the Lord? But what had been the case with Hagar, also a foreign woman, before Moses' law, was not the case with Ruth, after that law had been promulgated. For when Ruth resigned home, parents, and the gods of her youth, she joined herself with the children of Israel, out of devotion to Naomi, and was welcomed to do so not only by the people of Judah, but according to the Law, in which we repeatedly find the command to save the "virgins alike," even of those nations with whom the Israelites came into conflict, so that these women might be brought to the worship of the "one sole invisible God." And in the Prophets we read (Isa. 66: 3-8) that those of the stranger, whether male or female, who voluntarily accepted the covenants of the Lord and kept His sabbaths and appointed feasts and ordinances, even if they had been but eunuchs before, were to receive a place and name in His house, an everlasting name which would not be cut off; and their burnt offerings and sacrifices, the essential privilege of the Jews, would be accepted on God's altar. And in the Law, again, we find repeated injunctions concerning foreigners: "Love ye the stranger, for ye were strangers in the land of Egypt," etc. We see in the history of Ruth, that these injunctions were faithfully kept.

Ruth became an Israelite by adoption. Her filial devotion and reverence illustrated her acceptance of the Law and her obedience. That God selected a king whose ancestress was Moabitish cannot fairly be brought forward as an objection. If it were unlawful for any stranger to be joined with Israel, we should not find so many laws regarding the foreigner in the Mosaic code. Ruth's virtue and goodness rendered her worthy in the eyes of God and man; and that is the crux of the matter for the followers of the Hebrew religion.

We see, then, the dangers inherent in intolerance, for here was a woman who achieved virtue in the Israelite sphere, by dint of her loyal and affectionate nature. Were we to fall prey—as did Naomi for a moment, in her bitterness in Moab—to a fear of, and hatred for, the foreigner, then we would not only lose the boon of friendship, but we might also deflect one who could only enrich our own faith.

In Ruth's seed were all the nations of the earth blessed. From her were descended David, Daniel, and Jesus.

Manoah's Wife

After the death of Abdah, twelfth judge of Israel, "the children of Israel again did evil in the sight of the Lord, and He delivered them into the hands of the Philistines forty years." The deliverer of the Hebrews once again issued from a brave and intrepid woman.

In the tribe of Dan was a certain lord by the name of Manoah, whose wife was childless. God sent to this woman an angelic messenger, who bore not only the revelation of the Lord's will concerning a blessed offspring, but also instructions as to the food and drink she was to refrain from taking during pregnancy, and a command as to the babe's upbringing, which was to be in the righteousness of His cause.

The woman carried this information to her husband, who was astonished, but who believed in her. Theirs seems to have been a trusting union, and though they had, like so many Israelites, grown distant from the laws of Moses and his tabernacle, they were of one heart in bending down in prayer to the One God: "Then Manoah entreated the Lord, and said, O my Lord, let the man of God which Thou didst send come again to us, and teach us what we shall do unto the child that shall be born."

Scripture continues: "And God hearkened to the voice of Manoah." The Lord sent again his messenger to reiterate the instructions. Manoah and his wife listened carefully, and piously accepted their mission. Their simplicity was such that they were ignorant of the divinity of the messenger, however, and they offered him hospitality. And the angel of the Lord said unto Manoah, "Though thou detain me, I will not eat of thy bread: and if thou wilt offer a burnt offering, thou must offer it unto the Lord."

For Manoah knew not that he was an angel of the Lord. And Manoah said, What is thy name, that when thy sayings come to pass we may do thee honor? And the angel of the Lord said unto him, Wherefore asketh thou thus after my name, seeing it is secret? So Manoah took a kid with a meat-offering, and offered it upon a rock unto the Lord. And it came to pass, when the flame went up toward heaven from off the altar, the angel of the Lord ascended in the flame of the altar, and Manoah and his wife looked on it, and fell with their faces to the ground. And the angel of the Lord did no more appear unto Manoah and his wife. Then Manoah knew he was an angel of the Lord. And Manoah said, We shall surely die, for we have seen God. But his wife said unto him, If the Lord were pleased to kill us, He would not have received a burnt-offering and a meat-offering at our hands, neither would He have showed us all these things, nor would as at this time have told us such things as these.

That the angel directed the couple's attention towards God, and away from himself, illustrates vividly the inroads of foreign faiths upon the Hebrew law; for even this chosen pair would have worshiped the messenger and not God. But even in their simplicity, they strained for the devout manner, and did as they were bidden. When they viewed at first hand the power of God, they were awed and overwhelmed; their simplicity again came to the fore when they feared death for having encountered the godhead.

Their equality as man and wife is evident, their confidence in one another unflagging. And even though cast down into a foreign faith, they were able to rise together to reclaim the beliefs of their fathers.

And though Manoah took the initiative when God's messenger reappeared, as was customary in his position as husband, nevertheless it was to his wife that the Lord first communicated His will. Manoah must have understood the favored position of his spouse, for he was careful to include her in all he said. In the religious observance of the burnt offering, and in the lowly prostration with which they acknowledged the divine power, Manoah and his wife were separately named, proving her complete equality in the Hebrew faith and her God-given right to that position. Manoah feared for both himself and the woman, as responsible agents possessing free will. And the very demonstrativeness of the wife in quickly deciphering the Lord's true intentions was a testament not only to her wit—and it was wit indeed in those dark times—but to her ready independence. She had been awestruck, like her husband, but was the first to comprehend the true meaning of the revelation.

Though the tribe of Dan had drifted from the laws of Moses, still it is evident that the family structure, and the disposition of familial responsibility, remained essentially as Moses had defined it. That Manoah's wife could both comprehend and judge, freely, the divine event, implies a domestic and social position which not only permitted but encouraged the lawful independence of the wife.

Manoah's actions toward his wife indicate that one did not dictate to the other, but influenced, in his own way, the actions of the other. There is a touching gentleness in their connubial relations, and if it was the woman who was quicker, it was not a bone of contention between them. Manoah's wife was forthright throughout, in her dealings with her God and with her husband, and fearless before the will of the Lord. Certainly it was a time so dense with false faith that we can only marvel at this woman's devotion and unremitting fortitude. She was well chosen to be the mother of Samson.

Delilah

We encounter, in the Old Testament, women of such varied character that we may truly say of the Scriptures that they provide a profoundly rich vein of human, particularly female, diversity. We have seen, thus far, revered priestesses and prophetesses, humble housewomen and workers, mothers and wives; Egyptian, Moabitess, and Midianite; the ambitious and simple, the submissive and rebellious, the deceiving and the devoted. From high station to low, from positions of power to those of utter subjection, from many lands and faiths, the women of the Old Testament, whether in the person of Miriam or of Deborah, of Hagar or of Bithya, of Rachel or of Ruth, are drawn, each and every one, with a skillful pen that neither simplifies nor caricatures. We might almost say that the inspired authors of the Old Testament wrote not with a pen, but painted, rather, with a brush, painted with many hues and colors, catching in the muscular, yet evocative, biblical style the many shades of human character.

All the women whose stories we have examined were presented with moral choices which, one way or another, for good or ill, they strove to make. Only in the cases of Deborah, Jephthah's daughter, and Ruth do we find the brush gleaming with sparkling colors unalloyed by darker shades; for the most part, biblical women were both virtuous *and* sinful, with the onus depending, I suppose, upon one's interpretation; indeed, the interpretations are so various that they testify to the complexity of vision which the Bible embodies.

For instance, we may wrinkle our brow over Rachel's cunning webs, which she spun with all the shrewdness in her nature; on the other hand, we may protest that she made Jacob very happy with her affectionate ways, and that she loved him dearly, for all her intricate designs, for all her envious, sacrilegious actions. We may say that Emtelai was heartless, because she left her babe so long exposed; yet it was an awful time, and she made her choice under circumstances that would try the soul of any man or woman. We may judge Sarah as imperious and jealous, but she acted in what she conceived to be the best interests of her line. Likewise, many find Hagar's spite and pride objectionable; yet she had been placed into slavery by (from her standpoint) foreign hands, only to be cast out when her usefulness to those same foreigners was over. And we might go on drawing illustrations of the diverse facets of feminine character and condition found in the Old Testament.

Splashes of light and dark smears, livid passions and subdued patience, and grey areas of ambiguity—of such is the canvas on which woman's nature is represented in the Bible. And so it is, too, with the biblical relations between women and men. There is the submissiveness of Leah to Jacob coexisting with the wily sorcery of Rachel. There is the intimate equality of Manoah and his wife, each contributing to the other's strength. Zipporah stands unresponsive and distant from her husband, Moses. There is the overwhelming love of daughter for father in Jephthah's tale, and of a sister's love for her brother in Miriam's. And in the history of Eve all love between the sexes is concentrated, from the paradise of affection to the hell of duty, from the wisdom of love to the affliction of love's bondage. The spectacle of human love, in its many and complex forms, comprises, indeed, one of the Bible's major themes. For love may draw together as well as tear asunder; it may ennoble as well as degrade; it may be meet in the sight of the Lord and according to moral judgment, or it may be ungodly, sinful, and selfish. Love may be as pure as that of Ruth for Naomi or as sullied as Dinah's. The Old Testament gives us love, in its many and varied forms, with the same all-encompassing insight that infuses the book as a whole. Archetypical, and for that very reason relevant to modern times, the Bible pours out its tales of women coupled with their men in eternal devotion, deception, and despair. The stories are spare and forceful, and yet subtle. Was not Jacob enslaved by Rachel while he struggled to do God's will? And was not Rebekah capable of great love, though she favored her second son? Did not Tamar deceive at the very moment she claimed her rightful love? We may be quick to judge, but the Bible is not; for it expresses the fulsome experiences of humanity, and in the recounting of those experiences does not damn outright, but *witnesses* in its profound wisdom.

And so it is with the tale of Delilah.

This woman, who was Samson's undoing, was not of the Hebrews but of the Philistines, their oppressors. For this reason, perhaps, her name has become synonymous with the deceitful seductress, the unprincipled schemer, the lewd wanton. For she was a foreign woman whose interests were antithetical to those of the Jews. Because of her patriotic feelings, then, she has come to be considered a "snare," like the very gods of the nations that were in conflict with Israel. The simple verses describing her give us a picture of a beautiful, but hard, woman; still, she never claimed to be other than a Philistine. It was Samson's own weakness, not her negative power, that brought the giant low. This the Old Testament makes clear, and she is never seen—this "evil destroyer," as some would have it—as anything more or less than what she ought to have been. She is a type, to be sure, and used Samson for her own ends; but we have already seen glimmerings of such a type in Rachel and Miriam, both of whom misused their power; and if Delilah was a destroyer, then it is evident that she considered Samson to be no less so. Theirs was an excessive passion between almost natural enemies, and no good could possibly have come of it, no matter what the character of Delilah. As the Philistines oppressed the Jews, so did Samson, in his strength, threaten the Philistines. The tale of their ill-favored love is set against the backdrop of war in this dark period of the judges.

Samson, son of Manoah and his wife, was a hero to his people, the last judge but one. He made successful war against his nation's oppressors and was a symbol of fearsome resistance to those who would enslave the followers of Abraham and Moses. He stands out in sharp relief in the Bible by virtue of his immense strength; he seems also to have asked very little for himself and to have been wholeheartedly committed to the cause of his people.

In order to form some idea of the great fear in which the

Philistines held Samson we have only to consider some of the legends which grew up around this massive figure. For instance, in Ginzberg we read:

> Samson's strength was superhuman, and the dimensions of his body were gigantic—he measured sixty ells between the shoulders.... The first evidence of his gigantic strength he gave when he uprooted two great mountains, and rubbed them against each other. Such feats he was able to perform as often as the spirit of God was poured out over him. Whenever this happened, it was indicated by his hair. It began to move and emit a bell-like sound, which could be heard far off. Besides, while the spirit rested upon him, he was able with one stride to cover a distance equal to that between Zorah and Eshtaol.*

Little wonder, then, that the Philistines might search in vain for some method of conquering this enormous presence. They could not meet him upon the battlefield, for he was an infantry unto himself (and a fine general besides); they shrank from him as if he were, in fact, a natural disaster, an act of God, like an earthquake or flood. He was delivering his people from their bondage, and there was nothing, apparently, that the Philistines could do about it.

Matters continued thus for some time, with the impotence of the Philistines growing more and more evident. *They* could not stop Samson; only Samson could do that.

And this he did, by way of a passion that burns across the pages of the Old Testament. We have encountered the lusts of the body in the Rabelaisian tale of Tamar and Judah and in the fondness Jacob felt for the lovely Rachel. But here the passion was more than momentary and less than lawful. It was not returned by Delilah, this all-consuming passion, and in Samson's last, humiliating days we see that perhaps he did not care whether she reciprocated his feelings or not. He underwent an infatuation and a folly as great as his own physical body, and cared only for the pleasure he could get from Delilah. There is nothing in this tale that suggests Samson

---

*See Ginzberg, p. 523.

deserved any better treatment than he received.

Samson fell in love with this Philistine woman at first glance, and after *only* a glance. Without hesitation, he set about procuring her.

> I have seen a woman in Timnath, of the daughters of the Philistines; therefore get her for me for a wife. Then said his father and his mother, Is there never a woman of the daughters of thy people, that thou goest to take a Philistine woman to wife? But he said, Get her for me; for she pleaseth me well.

Manoah and his wife spoke to their son with wisdom, but he would have none of it. Delilah was brought to the household of Samson, against her will, but already devising a plan by which to fell the rude giant. The Philistine leaders told Delilah, "Entice thy husband that he may declare unto us the riddle [of his great strength]." For Samson chose *to play* with his wife, knowing well her antipathy for his nation. Perhaps it amused him to tell riddles over which Delilah and her cohorts would ponder in vain. It is the picture of a great child torturing insects that both amuse and revolt him. It is little wonder that Delilah came to despise him.

> And Samson's wife wept before him, and said, Thou dost but hate me, and lovest me not; thou hast put forth a riddle unto the children of my people, and hast not told me. And she wept before him seven days, and on the seventh day he told her.

And what he told her was, of course, a lie. He continued to toy with his enemies, and with his own fate, simply for the sexual pleasure he took from Delilah. Finally, detesting this man who was using *her* to at least the same extent as she was using *him*, she arranged to have herself spirited home, whereupon Samson declared war on the Philistines. There follows the record of Samson's great exploits in this war, and the terrible price the Philistines paid for Delilah's return. Needless to say, Samson got back his foreign wife; it is just as needless to say, that she resumed her former position with the same deep resolve to bring the giant to heel.

Delilah worked upon the man's weakest instincts. Cajoling,

lascivious, she wheedled herself into his affections, and tyrannized over his sexuality. This animal power was all she possessed, and she used it to the utmost of her capacity.

"How canst thou say, I love thee," she asked him, "when thy heart is not with me? Thou hast mocked me... and hast not told me wherein thy great strength lieth." And it came to pass when she pressed him daily with her words, and urged him so that his soul was vexed to death, that he told her all his heart.

We know from Ginzberg's account (quoted above) that Samson placed great importance on his locks of hair, which were the harbingers of the Lord's will when the Spirit was upon him. Without those locks he feared that God would not favor him, and this he conveyed to Delilah. She was quick to exploit these fears in her husband.

She at once contacted her people:

She sent and called the lords of the Philistines, saying, Come up this once, he hath told me all his heart. And she made him sleep upon her knees; and called for a man, and bade him shave off the seven locks, and his strength went from him. And she said, The Philistines be upon thee, Samson, and he awoke and said, I will go out and shake myself, as at other times, and he wist not that the Lord was departed from him. But the Philistines took him, and put on him fetters of brass, and he did grind in their prison house.

Ginzberg recounts* that Samson continued to behave in a profligate manner even in prison, finding himself the plaything of those with whom he had only recently toyed. Blinded, degraded, he parted life with an entreaty to his God, that he should be able to see better in the next world. Let us hope he did.

As for Delilah, nothing more is said of her. She had accomplished

---

*See Ginzberg, p. 523.

her mission, received her reward, and cared not to look upon Samson again.

A crude man and a cruel woman—such were Samson and Delilah. The Bible witnesses their folly with a remarkably stark and penetrating gaze. Nothing of Samson's great services to his people is gainsaid; neither are we deflected by our admiration for his strength and devotion from recognizing that there coexisted in his nature a sensual compulsion which he could not master. Though he might carry the gates of Gaza upon his back, he could not bear the responsibility for his own passions. He demanded nothing from his people in return for his tremendous feats of courage; and yet, like a child, he would grab at the first bauble that struck his eye, and demanded, not homage, but his nation's patience with his dangerous whims. Steadfast in the Israelite cause, in his own cause he wavered. Not even his parents could deflect his single-minded, self-destructive obsession with a foreign woman's flesh. And thus, because he betrayed himself, he also betrayed his people's cause.

And the woman who was his instrument in this betrayal was not of the Hebrews. As was the case with Hagar, it must be realized that she was brought against her will into foreign hands; unlike Hagar, of course, Delilah had no love for any among the Jews. Though this hatred she scarcely concealed, we may say that she was cold. She took upon herself the role of temptress and betrayer, and did so with relish. But as the Old Testament recounts, she had no choice in the matter of her removal, once Samson had laid eyes upon her. She did not seek to be his wife, and bore no feeling for his religion. She had the choice, then, of betraying him or of remaining submissive to him, an enemy of her kind, who used her as a mere sexual object. May we conclude, then, that she was totally unjustified in her actions? The Old Testament does not.

Rather, the biblical verses give witness to the fact that Delilah's evil, in this dread tale, consisted not in her behavior towards Samson, but in her political wrongdoing. She scorned patience with, or understanding of, the oppressed Israelites. Like all the nations who battled the Hebrews, hers extended no love nor help to other peoples. The dark, bloody period in which her story is set bespeaks the truly revolutionary character of the Mosaic tolerance of foreigners, for in the days of the judges fear and distrust were everywhere rampant. Delilah was completely of her nation in despising those they bound in slavery.

But as to her *character,* that, these verses show, was inevitable, given the fact that Samson rudely snatched her from her own kind and extended, after all, no respect for her, as a woman or as a Philistine. It was as if, by Samson's own actions, the Mosaic law were set at naught, and all Delilah's most negative tendencies utterly confirmed. She was taken for a slave—though Samson called her his wife—by those she had been brought up to think of as slaves. To betray Samson was, in her mind, tit for tat.

Hannah

Near Mount Ephraim a man called Elkanah lived with his two wives, Hannah and Peninnah. Remarkably enough, this is the first instance since the time of Jacob that a man is reported to have had more than one wife. Joseph, Moses, Othniel, and Manoah all took but one woman for a wife, each in his own time, which gives rise to the supposition that polygamy, though permitted, was not necessarily a factor in family policy. Even before the period of the monarchy, Israel was, as we have seen, in utter disarray, but in respect of family stability the basic household unit seems to have been strengthened, if anything. The occasion for polygamy arose in times when the population of the Hebrew nation was imperiled, fell to nothing when the population grew to great proportions, and arose again when the basically egalitarian structure of Jewish society diminished under the monarchy. In the case of Elkanah and his wives, we see an early example of the re-emergence of polygamy; but since the monarchy had yet to be established, we see also that it was bound, this ancient tradition, by strict laws.

"And Elkanah, with his wives and household, went up out of his city yearly to worship and sacrifice unto the Lord in Shiloh." Shiloh was then the place of God's holy ark, and of His priests. At such times, "he gave to Peninnah his wife, and to all her sons and daughters, portions, but unto Hannah he gave a double portion; for he loved Hannah: though the Lord had not granted her any children." Elkanah loved Hannah as Jacob loved Rachel, for her own self, although Hannah's virtues we may count as a trifle more consistent than Rachel's, and worthier, perhaps, of her husband's great love.

In Israel, as in all ancient nations, the denial of children was considered a sad reproach. It must have affected Hannah, however much love her husband heaped upon her. And Hannah's grief was painfully aggravated by the provocations of her more fecund rival, whose unkind reproaches increased with every year that diminished Hannah's hopes for motherhood. As the more beloved by her husband, Hannah might have told him of these continual provocations, for she would have been assured of her husband's interference and protection; she chose, however, not to alienate Peninnah from her husband and cause domestic strife. It was easier for her to suffer than to complain.

Each visit to Shiloh excited again Peninnah's reproaches; and since this took place some years before Elkanah noticed the grief of his favorite wife, we may in some degree suppose that Hannah's endurance was extensive. Hers was no trial of a day or a month, but of years; and there is nothing more trying to the spirit than living with one whose tongue is bitter and lacerating. "Peninnah provoked her sore, to make her fret," the Bible says, and provoked her for no fault of her own.

Visits to Shiloh must have been heavy with suffering to Hannah. It was not only the signal of Peninnah's cruelty, but the very sight of all her countrymen flocking to the ark, with their show of sons and daughters, must have made her own heart shrink in woe. She felt that the Lord had forsaken her; still, she did not complain aloud or make a show of her grief. For instance, we read of Elkanah's gentle reproofs: "Hannah, why weepest thou? why eatest thou not? and why is thy heart grieved? Am not I better to thee than ten sons?"

Here there is no reference to anything but Hannah's visible sorrow and to Elkanah's supposition as to the cause of her grief. And in accordance with the enduring beauty of her character, Hannah makes no complaining answer. Elkanah's words reveal the extent and truth of his love; and had it not been for the daily provocations of Peninnah, he might indeed have been to Hannah "better than ten sons," but she had griefs and trials of which he knew nothing, and these, in childlike faith and prayer, she communicated to her God.

The condition of married women among the Jews, in the time of the judges, must have been independent and unrestrained, as we have noted in the tale of Manoah's wife. We find Hannah rising up after they had eaten and drunk in Shiloh, and without even imparting her intentions to her husband, much less asking his consent, going completely unattended and unrebuked to the temple of her God. There, in bitterness of soul, she prayed to Him; and, in accordance with the Mosaic law, which provided for such emergencies, she vowed that if the Eternal would in His infinite mercy remember His handmaid, and grant her a male child, she would devote him to God all the days of her life, and not a razor should come near his head.

But she did not pray aloud, nor according to any ritual; she prayed merely as her heart dictated: "She spoke in her heart," as Scripture puts it. Only her lips moved, but her voice was not heard. And Eli, the high priest, who sat beside one of the posts of the temple, marked her mouth, and hearing no word, combined with Hannah's agitation, believed her to be drunk, and reproachfully ordered her to put her wine from her.

It must have been aggravating to find herself so misunderstood by one she believed would demand no explanation of her. She might have expected him to proffer relief, or offer solace instead. Still we find nothing in her gracious reply to suggest a failing in the firm faith which brought her in there.

No, my lord, I am a woman of a sorrowful spirit; I have drunk neither wine nor strong drink, but have poured out my soul before the Lord. Count not thine handmaid for a daughter of Belial; for out of the abundance of my grief and complaint have I spoken hitherto. Then Eli answered and said, Go in peace, and the God of Israel grant thee thy petition that thou hast asked of Him.

Hannah replied, "Let thine handmaid find grace in thy sight," meaning, remember her in his prayers, and then "she went her way, and did eat, and her countenance was no more sad."

At the conclusion of the festival, Elkanah and his family returned to their city, where the Eternal remembered his faithful servant, and taking from her the reproach of her peers, in due course of time granted her the son for which she had so earnestly prayed; and in joyful acknowledgment that it was in answer to her prayer that this son had been given her, she called him Samuel, or "asked of the Lord."

The time again came round for Elkanah and his family to make their yearly offerings in Shiloh. Hannah had imparted to her husband the vow she had made concerning their offspring, and Elkanah wholeheartedly endorsed it. They went together to the temple to confirm it. And on the day after their visit to the temple, they rose up in the morning early, and "worshipped before the Lord." This was a token of thanksgiving and rejoicing on both their parts: on Elkanah's, that his beloved wife was no longer sad; on Hannah's that her prayer was heard.

Hannah, however, when the time of the yearly sacrifice arrived, refused to go up, saying to her husband, "I will not go up till the child is weaned; and then I will bring him, that he may appear before the Lord, and there abide forever." Her husband approved this resolution. "Do what seemeth thee good," he replied; "Tarry until thou hast weaned him."

Again, we see the equality existing between husband and wife under the Mosaic law. That women as well as men were to appear in the house of the Lord, and join in His worship, is proved by both

Hannah and Peninnah: they and their children attended the husband in his worship. Hannah tarried, because to go up three times a year was a restriction only binding upon males due to the many circumstances which might prevent females, particularly mothers, from doing so.

The time at length came when, in obedience to her voluntary vow, Hannah had to part from her child and deliver him into the service of God. The child Samuel was precious beyond belief to Hannah, and yet she showed no hesitation, no thought of delay, no forgetfulness, and no faltering in delivering him up, even though no one but her husband knew of her vow, not even the high priest, who had promised that her prayer would be granted without knowing what it was. She had maternal anxieties, surely; but when the child was weaned, she took him with her to Shiloh, with offerings from the store, the field, and the vineyard, all in exact accordance with the law. Coming into the house of the Lord, she said to Eli, "O my lord, as thy soul liveth, my lord, I am the woman that stood by thee here praying unto the Lord. For this child I prayed, and the Lord hath given me my petition which I asked of Him, and therefore also have I lent him to the Lord: as long as he liveth he shall be lent to the Lord. And he worshipped the Lord there," meaning that Eli acknowledged His goodness in giving the woman what she had desired more than anything else on earth.

The prayer, or hymn, of thanksgiving which Hannah poured fourth contains evidence of her great gratitude, couched in strains of the sublime poetry. As in the tales of Miriam and Deborah, we find here a vivid token of the intellectual heights of the Israelite woman, a token which confirms the high station of women in Hebrew social structure. The intellects of these women must have been of a high order, for the facility with which they transformed their aspirations into exquisite words proves how completely poetry infused their lives. Poetry is one of the ultimate forms of culture, and the freedom with which such women as Miriam and Deborah and Hannah used this form gives some idea of the cultural place of women among the Hebrews, and a clear illustration of the Hebrew female's intellectual gifts. Since we have dwelt upon the poetic flights of Miriam and

Deborah, we take the liberty of quoting Hannah's magnificent lines in full:

> My heart rejoiceth in Jehovah,
> My horn is exalted in Jehovah;
> My speech shall flow out over my enemies,
> Because I rejoice in Thy salvation.
> There is none holy as Jehovah:
> For there is none beside Thee:
> Neither is there any rock like our God.
> Talk no more so exceeding proudly;
> Let not arrogance come out of thy mouth:
> For Jehovah is a God of knowledge,
> By Him are actions weighed.
> The bows of mighty men are broken,
> But the weak are girded with strength.
> The rich have hired out for bread;
> But the hungry cease from want.
> The barren woman hath borne seven;
> The fruitful one hath grown feeble.
> Jehovah killeth and maketh alive;
> He bringeth down to the grave and bringeth up.
> Jehovah maketh poor and maketh rich;
> He bringeth low, and lifteth up.
> He raiseth the poor out of the dust,
> He lifteth the beggar from the dunghill,
> To set them among princes,
> To make them inherit the throne of glory;
> For the pillars of the earth are Jehovah's,
> He hath set the world upon them.
> He will keep the feet of his saints,
> The wicked shall be silent in darkness;
> For by strength no man shall prevail.
> The adversaries of Jehovah shall be broken to pieces;
> Out of heaven shall He thunder upon them.
> Jehovah shall judge the ends of the earth;

> He shall give strength unto His king,
> And exalt the horn of His anointed.

There is fire, profound insight, and fervent faith in these lines. We hear a woman's voice raised up in both wisdom and ecstasy. There is no conceit or self-exaltation in her song of praise, no supposition of her own worth or uniqueness. All is on a universal plane; all and everything comes from Him. It was He who made bare His arm, He who gave the barren children, and strength to those who stumbled, while the mighty He broke and the rich He humbled. Men will be brought low, men will be lifted up, but "by strength no man shall prevail." This song is the summation of faith in a Being whose hand fell upon all equally, and who bestowed his blessings not for the sake of the powerful but in the interests of the loving, the pious and the meek. In our dark age—darker even than the days of the judges, perhaps—we look askance at what we consider naivete in these lines, for it may often seem to us that no hand helps the downtrodden or the weak, who appear to us bereft of an omnipotent protector. But our age, too, shall come to an end, and those without faith will find it trying, indeed, to face the chaos that threatens us. Neither dictator nor rich man can escape the disintegration of entire societies. It is on this universal level that Hannah intended her words; and certainly no naivete can, upon examination of these lines, be imputed to her. She lived in an unsettled time, had been plagued with self-doubts, and had been ill-used and spitefully treated by others. Yet she was able to love, and inspire love, and able to look with intelligence, compassion, intuition, and righteousness upon the generality of her kind, and to consign to her God the disposition of justice, in the deepest and most painfully purchased faith. She believed *because* she was intelligent, not because she was simple or obtuse. She had reflected on her own history, and had looked about her at the world, and had seen that the downtrodden, too, might be lifted up, and the powerful deposed. No finer testament to woman's wisdom can be found than these words of Hannah's; for by faith, she tells us, all trials may be borne, and by faith all vicissitude defined, so that one may remain whole—and ultimately triumphant—in the midst of darkness and chaos.

She must have been sad indeed to leave her boy at the temple and return to her home, knowing full well that she would see him but three times a year, as was the law. But this she accepted as she had accepted the boy's birth: with faith that from her sacrifice would come great good. And in Samuel, of course, we see this good realized.

Through the conduct of the high priest's sons, treachery and licentiousness had crept into the realm of God's temple. Yet in the midst of bad faith and under the lax guidance of Eli, the child Samuel kept as undefiled a nature as was his mother's.

Although the awful conduct of Eli's sons was well known, Hannah did not seem to entertain a fear as to the effect of their example upon the youth of her son. She had experienced the effects of faith too deeply to begin doubting now, and she continued, it is certain, to offer prayers that he might become what he was intended to be. She neither regretted nor reproached herself for the giving of her son to God's service, for no matter how low the temple fell she knew that it was God who would dispose justice.

Every time she visited Shiloh, Hannah brought a little coat or robe for her boy, the work of her own hands, and the product of her fidelity and fond hopes. Eli blessed Elkanah and his wife, and said, "The Lord give thee seed of this woman, for the loan which is lent to the Lord." In the fullness of time, Hannah was granted three more sons and two daughters, proving to her that the Eternal returned double, and more so, for that which she had devoted to him. And what she had devoted was intelligence, simple faith, and prayer.

After imparting the information that Hannah mothered five children, the Scriptures close around the sterling figure of the woman; but knowing the longevity of biblical characters, we might infer that she was spared to experience in full the happiness which her firstborn's matured character brought to the Hebrew nation.

From his earliest childhood, Samuel seems not to have faltered in his faith, and to have carried on the devotion of his mother. We read of his unvarying integrity and obedience to God, from his first repetition to Eli of the Lord's awful sentence to the very end of his life. This obedience and unwavering honesty—the inheritance from Hannah—often interfered with his own private feelings, first towards Eli, then towards Saul; but he always followed the dictates of his faith. It may truly be said that in Samuel, Hannah received her due—more than that, she had given to God His due.

This history we have been examining is so fraught with importance to women that we might pause to dwell upon it for a time. Strongly as the stories of Miriam and Deborah marked the real position of the Israelite woman, and proved their powers of intellect, judgment, and spirit, as well as the deferential light in which they were regarded by their countrymen, the history of Hannah brings their freedom and equality, even in the marriage state, yet more distinctly to light. Deborah was inspired to do the will of the Lord. She was gifted extraordinarily and expressly to judge and deliver her nation from foreign bondage. Naomi, as a widow, was unhampered by either social or household restraints, and was free to proceed as she chose. Hannah was one of two wives, her husband living, and the head of a large household; consequently, she had her part to perform in the daily flow of things; still, she was not bound in the least in her temporal or spiritual feelings. She did not ask her husband's acquiesence, much less depend upon his consent to seek the house of God. Her very going to pray would have excited remark if such had not been the common custom of the nation. And if women were not permitted to pray for themselves, Eli would have rebuked her and asked her to send her husband to the temple, telling her that only then would her wishes be granted; instead of which, when once convinced of her earnestness and sorrow, he bade her "go in peace," and told her that God would listen to her.

Again, had she not possessed freedom of will and action, she could not have vowed her child to God. Unless she had been perfectly sure that her husband had sufficient confidence in her to abide by her decision, she could not have so committed him, without mocking her God, by making a promise which she had not the power to perform.

Elkanah was completely secondary in Hannah's story. It was the wife who brought and offered the bullocks, flower, and wine provided for the offering; the wife who addressed Eli; the wife who chanted the splended song of praise to her God; and the wife who devoted her child to his service. The husband and father had not more to do with the matter of Samuel than to make the simple acts of acquiescence and approval, which he would not have so unhesitatingly bestowed, had he not possessed the most perfect confidence in the judgment and behavior of his wife.

That no severe restrictions as to time, form, or words of prayer existed in the time of the judges is proved by Hannah's seeking the Temple to pray when it was not the appointed time of service, and there was no one there but the high priest and her, and by her speaking from the heart and in her heart the words which sorrow and desperation dictated, without any regard whatever to instituted forms of worship, which might have stifled her outpourings.

That rigorous forms of prayer were not needed in those times is a testament to the self-knowledge of the people. Silent prayer in the sight of God is illustrative of a person's understanding with regard to his or her true motives and to the eternal order of things. Individual prayer gives breath to religion, for it marks the spiritual freedom in which individuals exist and the responsibility which such freedom carries. Before another—before judge or witness—one may easily lie. But what is the benefit of lying silently, in solitude before God? It is an internal act which bares one's own soul and offers it to a greater power.

It was thus that Hannah came to Him, trusting Him, even more than she trusted or confided in her husband, who was her closest earthly tie. She did not think herself too unworthy to approach and beseech Him, because she knew that the law which she obeyed, and the whole history of her people, abounded with His invitation to pray and His promise to answer. She came to Him because she knew He loved her, and would have compassion; and because she so loved Him, it was easier to pour into His ear her mute sorrows than to breathe them to a man. She came to Him, too, because she believed in Him with such a pure and childlike, yet profoundly intelligent, faith that when the high priest told her "go in peace, and God grant thee thy petition," she returned to her home calmly, trustingly, and "did eat, and her countenance was no more sad." These words are convincing as to how fully she must have believed when she prayed, and not only then, but throughout her lifetime; for faith develops, not from feeling only, but from long and careful reflection. Her simple gifts, which she carried to Samuel thrice yearly in the Temple, show a developing strength of faith, despite the licentiousness which she knew was infecting the Lord's place. But she saw Samuel grow and mature and become wise, and did not fret herself with the possibility of his falling prey to bad faith. She knew that his individual soul was infused with God's will, just as hers had been when she pronounced the beautiful and renowned song of praise. And even if Samuel had fallen, her faith would not have been shaken, for she understood the rise and fall of man's history and the omnipotent wisdom that broods upon it. Her faith was in acceptance and in trust, and it is to her that we owe one of the most enthralling expressions of religious passion ever uttered.

Hannah confirms the importance of individual prayer while, in her song, placing the individual in his or her proper place in the universe—in the all-seeing gaze of God. Such individual faith as she symbolizes is needed in order to discern the workings of an eternal Love and infinite Goodness in man's history. Man is linked with God in the same manner as the tides with the moon, or upheaval with the inscrutable winds. God is the center for man through all his toil and rage, revolution and pain, war and disaster; for man's actions, in whatever event, are measured against Him and watched over by Him, so that his behavior is not so much bleating in a void, or so much crying in a vacuum. Hannah understood that the standard and heart of man's history was in God, and that, finally, nothing could be understood or accepted without reference to Him.

Simple faith and great understanding—such were the hallmarks of Hannah's character. She showed fortitude and patience, but through all her trials absorbed the lessons of life and the law of her God. And she transformed her knowledge into poetry that even the wisest of scholars marvel at, and the most accomplished of word-masters thrill to the sound of. She was a simple woman who combined her experience with her reason, her faith with her suffering, and there is no greater amalgram that this of the philosophic and poetic temper.

Of course, Samuel did not try his mother's devotion: he was the last and most beloved of Israel's judges. One of the finest passages in the Bible describes his character well, even as a child. Lamps burned in the temple, and the boy Samuel was awakened by a mysterious voice, calling him to the knowledge of His power and love. The boy was not so much awed as full of wonder, and in his innocence responded wholeheartedly to the gentle commands of his God. Old Eli, naturally, could not at first believe that the boy had witnessed God, but by slow perception came to realize the significance of this child. For already the prophetic powers and wisdom of a judge were radiating from Samuel, and in his long career he was never once to waver in the true course of faith which was his mother's legacy.

———*Ichabod's Mother*———

Eli, priest of the temple at Shiloh, with whom we have met in the tale of Hannah, had, as we noted in that tale, two wicked sons. One of them, Phinehas, was particularly avaricous and degenerate. Both he and his brother "lay with the women that assembled at the door of the tabernacle of the congregation," and the long-suffering wife of Phinehas witnessed not only the crimes of her husband but the stealing of the sacred ark by the Philistines, mainly through the negligence of this same husband.

She is credited, this woman, upon the theft of the ark, with these words: "The glory is departed from Israel: because the ark of God was taken." She seems to have been a devout woman in a dark time, and she gave in completely to despair, at childbirth, when she heard of her husband's death in battle, and she died while delivering the ill-fated Ichabod.

Hers is, then, one of the truly unrelieved tragedies of the Old Testament.

—Nazbat and the Slave Girl—

Jesse, father of David, was a good man, a man of profound learning and high character, a man whose piety makes him one of the most memorable of the Bible's characters. And yet this scholar, whose moral exegeses and insights into Hebrew law were so highly regarded, was, after all, only a man.

In this early period of the monarchy, slaves were held, not as Abraham held Hagar in the days of the patriarchs, out of shared devotion, with no social opprobrium laid upon the rank of handmaiden, but as household possessions, who might be used as objects, though not, as in modern times, as barter. There were slaves in Jesse's household, as his was a prosperous and royal one, and once did he fall to contemplating one of his human possessions as a mere receptacle for his lust. The girl was a young handmaiden to Jesse's wife, Nazbat. She was a beautiful child and excited Jesse's desires, much to the anger of the wife, who moved to prevent an affair which she considered shameful, as it indeed was, according to both law and custom.

Had not Nazbat done so, no barrier would have prevented Jesse from exercising his will in this matter. Human sexual passion, as we have seen in Tamar's story, was often administered to by harlots—among the Jews as among all other peoples, in every time and place. But to use a handmaiden as a harlot was not lawful; still, that so good a man as Jesse intended to do so only indicates how common was such an outrage, and indicates as well the degeneration of the law at this time.

The intentions of Jesse were made known to Nazbat, probably by the slave girl herself, and this is how the wife foiled her husband:

At the appointed hour of the tryst, Nazbat disguised herself as the slave girl and met Jesse in the child's stead. Jesse was thoroughly taken in by this ruse, and as Judah before him, took his pleasure without regard for the woman who supplied it. He did, however, free the slave girl for her "services" to his "cause"; but Nazbat, having become pregnant during this ruse, feared that her deception might be uncovered, and—unlike Tamar—did not have the courage to confront the man with his own folly. So, upon its birth, she gave out the infant as the newly freed slave girl's own.

This infant, disinherited because of the unlawful lust of his father and the cowardice of his mother, was David.

No Rabelaisian humor lightens this tale, as is the case with Tamar's story. The deception encountered here was greater than that in the story of Judah and Tamar, where the law was recognized as underlying Tamar's droll means of obtaining her rights. Here, too, Nazbat's deception was lawful enough, given the circumstances, although, unlike Tamar, she had means at her disposal by which to confront her husband without resorting to ruse. We have seen already, in the tale of Manoah's wife, the equality existing between Hebrew marriage partners, and, certainly, given the pious and scholarly nature of Jesse, he would not have thought it amiss had Nazbat sought to reprove him, openly and to his face, on the basis of the law. The fact is, however, that the wife *feared* to do so. And thus we are met with the probability that, during this time, the degree of honesty between husband and wife had been adumbrated to notable extent. After all, the character of Jesse and Nazbat was in most ways exemplary; thus, we may measure the possibility of widespread deception among Hebrew marriages by their example, which was higher, no doubt, than most.

The monarchy brought, then, not only the reinstitution of polygamy to the Israelites, but an even more serious breakdown in marital relations: fear of husband by wife, and the use of household slaves for the sexual pleasure of the husband. Mosaic law had set down strict rules governing the respective rights of man and wife, and of servants, but these rules, though they existed still in form, do not seem during the monarchy, to have existed in spirit.

The Old Testament is the most subtle of moralists, simply *describing* as it does the historical rise and fall of Hebrew society. Just as the cruel king Saul would banish and kill, manipulate and take, according to his wanton moods, so would the nation of Israel show much moral incontinence during this monarchial period. And constantly, of course, there hangs over the history of the Israelites the examples of Abraham and Moses and Deborah, whose actions and promulgations must mock the lowest points of Jewish history, just as they symbolize the highest.

Equality, therefore, between husband and wife was to diminish under the monarchy. And Jesse's overpowering lust, despite the law, echoes that of Samson, though in Jesse's case the blame is more heavy, perhaps, as he was more profoundly aware of Hebrew tradition than Samson. Consequently, just as we note barriers arising between husband and wife, we note, too, in Jesse, a schism developing between the knowledge of eternal law and the whimsicality of sexual desire. Jesse's intellect and his body had, at this one point, gone different ways; and the slow, deliberate, lawful actions of Abraham towards Hagar, in that distant period of the patriarchs, were forgotten by Jesse in his attitude towards the slave girl. He was swept away by his own selfish lusts, and did not consult Nazbat openly, but conspired behind her back to have the slave girl.

Sarah, as we know, presided over the elevation of Hagar to the position of Abraham's second sife, and met honestly with her husband upon this matter. And Sarah did not fear to exercise her rights when she felt them to be threatened, and spoke up boldly to her husband upon such occasions. Nazbat seems to have been in no such position. She did not, probably, expect to become pregnant, and amplified her husband's shame by disowning the infant. And she increased the degree of marital deception.

The actions of both the mother and father in this tale were to have repercussions in the life of their son. But even more than the consequences, the *example* of their behavior serves as a summing up of the degenerative impulses extant in the period of the monarchy.

Abraham acted with probity and with respect in his dealings with Sarah, and in his attitude towards Hagar; Jacob never once faltered in his respect for Rachel, and in his regard for Bilhah and Zilpah; Judah acknowledged his mistakes openly and honestly in the matter of Tamar; towards Ruth Boaz showed not the least cruelty or impertinence. Obviously, during the monarchy these sterling examples no longer held such sway as standards of marital conduct, and in Nazbat, and her slave girl, at the hands of Jesse, we see the women of the household brought low, brought to a pretense and fear not countenanced by the generally proud history of Hebrew women.

Michal

There is not a great deal in the Old Testament concerning Michal, daughter of Saul, but what we have is remarkable, and points up the nature of royality during the monarchy.

The amount of love borne David by Michal throws a certain aura around the woman, for she must have suffered a great deal for her affections, especially in her youth, when her elder sister Merab was bethrothed to the future king of kings. It does not appear that Merab much loved David; but the younger daughter's love was apparently quite strong. For she pined for him when she knew he was intended for another, bewailed the fact that she had been set aside, and watched in mute despair as he chose one who cared not a whit for him. Even when this sorrow was removed by the union of Merab and Adriel—and the news of Michal's love for David mightily pleased her father, for he saw it as a means of entrapping the youth—she placed little confidence in her position, for she remembered how little truth there had been in the previous betrothal. Still, she was patient with her cruel father and open in her love towards David, and weathered the storms to become his first wife.

The love she bore the man must have continually exposed her to intense concern for his safety, for her father "grew yet the more afraid of David," and he repeatedly gave orders that he should be slain. Happily, he had taken his son Jonathan into his confidence, and the young man bravely came to his friend's defense, venturing even to call the king's intentions a sin against David, who had always done his duty, both to Saul and to his nation. For a time Jonathan's pleadings succeeded in mollifying the suspicious old man, and since David was again united with his king, as in the past, Michal's concerns must have subsided to some degree. But the young wife knew the briefest period of peace and conjugal happiness, for war with the Philistines again broke out.

David was always ready to die for his nation; Saul seems equally to have been ready to let him do so. But when David once again went out to fight the Philistines, and when he slew them so extensively that they fled from him, Saul only responded with hatred and set himself, once again, to the task of undoing his heroic son-in-law. Michal could not, therefore, even rejoice in her husband's valor, for she knew only too well the treachery and fears of her father, which would expose her young husband to renewed perils.

Even in the act of charming the monarch's jealous nature by playing so exquisitely on the harp, David was exposed to sudden death. While he played, Saul threw his javelin with such deadly aim that David escaped with his life only by darting quickly aside, and the spear broke against the wall. David fled the royal anger and returned to his home.

The danger was by no means over, however. For Saul had sent spies to watch over David's house and slay him upon his return. But David was so universally esteemed that information on the king's bloody intentions towards him was imparted to Michal, probably by the spies themselves—or perhaps by Jonathan, who was, like his sister, always on the alert for David's safety. In any case, Michal received these bleak tidings and told her husband: "Save thy life to-night, else to-morrow thou wilt be slain."

There is little in the way of hysterics in the character of Michal; she parted bravely and calmly from her husband, though she knew their parting might be for a lengthy period. Her anguish must have been intense, for twice the Scriptures have informed us that she "loved David"; but there was no wavering on her part in the matter of his safety. "She let him down through a window, and he went, and fled, and escaped." Michal, not daring to give way to strong emotion, busied herself in carrying out her strategem to obtain enough time for his escape, before he was pursued. She laid an image in David's bed, and put a pillow of goat's hair for his head, and covered it all with a cloth. When morning came, and Saul's messengers demanded David, she calmly told them he was sick; and with that information they promptly returned to their sovereign. The wrath of the king was not turned aside, and he commanded them: "Bring him up to me in the bed, that I may slay him." The messengers went back again, the wife's deception was exposed, and Michal was brought before her raging father.

"Wherefore hast thou deceived me so," he demanded, "and sent away mine enemy that he has escaped?"

To protect herself, Michal answered, "He said unto me, Let me go; why should I kill thee?"

This answer, in which is summed up all the wariness and fear that Michal felt concerning her father, seemed to satisfy the old man, at least so far as his daughter was concerned; but the search and pursuit of David continued without respite.

Michal was not to see her husband until he ascended the throne. During all this time, if she heard from him at all, she heard from him as a wanderer and exile, flying from place to place at the risk of his life. He had to contend with the hired assassins of Saul and was compelled to take refuge in the treacherous courts. At one time he was forced to hide in caves, in want of food and drink. Knowing the great love Michal bore David, these trails of his, when she heard of them, must have bitten deeply into her heart.

But the real bitterness was yet to come for Michal. For we are told that "Saul had given Michal, his daughter, David's wife, to Phalti, the son of Laish," an act of wanton tyranny on Saul's part, and in violation of the laws of Isarel. A divorce might permit a woman to become the wife of another man, but no divorce had taken place between Michal and her husband. Saul's actions proceeded from that determined persecution of David in which Saul indulged even to the point of setting God's laws at naught. Michal, of course, could not refuse her father and sovereign, but no slur is cast on her character. She cannot be blamed for obeying a command that it was possible for her to disobey only at her peril. "She loved David"—of this the Scriptures assure us. We know, then, that her acquiescence was not voluntary.

Saul had, then, become a tyrant even among his family. He had flung a javelin at his son Jonathan, just as he had at David, for Jonathan had continued to defend the future King. A man who might kill his own son for a simple, forthright defense of another, would not scruple to outrage his daughter's feelings by forcing her to marry a man she neither loved nor wanted. Saul, by this action, insulted David, and annulled the brief happiness that Michal had known as David's wife.

When David ascended to the throne, he restored Michal to himself. Thus, the iniquities of Saul, in the outrage of his daughter, were set to rights. David knew she was blameless, and did not choose to visit the father's sins upon the daughter. He recalled her to his heart and to his home, at the time when, had his spirit retained any enmity towards the house of Saul, he might have permitted her to remain neglected and uncared for in an equivocal station in Phalti's house.

Michal loved David, and believed in him as the future king. Her devotion did not, however, extend to all of her nation, and we are given, in the next mention of Michal, some idea of the woman's pride and her sense of her and her husband's position. It is not a story that reflects well on Michal's great capacity for love; but then, we must remember that she grew up among the royal household and was given, as a princess, the requisite amount of arrogance. Her love for David was a matter between equals on the social scale, and her quickness and energy in executing David's escape is proof enough that she loved the man exceedingly, for she risked her own life at the hands of an outraged father for so doing; but toward the generality of her countrymen she was not so well disposed. She was proud of her devotion to David, and would not see it shared with the people.

The story, then, is as follows. For twenty years the ark of God had remained in the house of Abinadab, whose son, Eleazer, had been sanctified to keep it. Through all the troubles of Saul's reign it had quietly remained there, Saul showing complete indifference to its sacred presence. David felt no such indifference, as the ark was to him unutterably holy, and he yearned for its influence. Therefore, every preparation was made to conduct the ark to Hebron, with all the ritual and honor that befitted its sanctity. Troubles, however, attended its journey, and the ark was given haven by the household of a Gittite. This Gittite family so prospered during the time in which they secured the ark that David, believing the sacred object to have the presence of the Lord within it, "went out and brought up the ark... to the city of David, with gladness."

A festival of rejoicing followed among the people of Hebron. Trumpets and holy songs marked its progress, and at every six paces oxen were offered to the Lord. David himself, shorn of all regal ornament, and dressed simply in a linen garment, joined with his whole heart in the solemn thanksgiving by dancing with his brethren before the Lord. Song and dance were, of course, modes of holy rejoicing for the Hebrews, and David was truly the king of his people in taking part. His simple manner of joining in also bespeaks a return to a more egalitarian state, obliterated under Saul. But this action on David's part did not please the daughter of Saul, who had herself, more than once, winced under the cruelty of the tyrant. She watched the proceedings with horror in her royal heart: "And as the ark came into the city of David, Michal, Saul's daughter, looked through a window and saw the king rejoicing.... And she despised him in her heart."

That King David, without any semblance of royalty or state, should mingle with the crowds, and become for the moment one of them, was too much for Michal's sensibility. He danced among them in lowly garments, and forgot, in his transport, that he was king over them—indeed, his intention seemed to be to erase all the barriers between royalty and commoner. That an egalitarian state was presupposed by the law of Moses did not slake the contempt which Michal felt upon this occasion. It was as if she herself were no more to David than the ruffians of the street, for he paraded himself without respect, as she felt, for the position of their household. The snobbery and haughtiness of a princess burned within her, and her once great warmth for David turned to ashes.

After the burnt offerings and peace offerings, David returned to bless his household; he was met by Michal, eager to give vent to her contempt: "How glorious was the king of Israel to-day, who uncovered himself in the eyes of the lowest of his servants, even as one of the vain fellows shamelessly uncovereth himself." Michal alludes here to the lowest class of people, who were obliged to remove their long upper garment so that it should not hinder them in their work. David had not, of course, literally uncovered himself; Michal's contempt takes the form here of a pun. She is attempting to needle David, to make him see that his actions placed him on a par with the most vulgar of his subjects.

> And David said unto Michal, It was before the Lord, which chose me before thy father, and before all his house, to appoint me ruler over the people of the Lord, over Israel: and therefore will I rejoice before the Lord. And I will yet be more vile than thus, and be base in my own sight: and of the maidservants of which thou hast spoken, shall I be had in honor.

This is a calm but emphatic reproof, and brings strongly before Michal the folly of her contempt. He asks, in effect, What are the trappings of state, the distinction of rank, before God? In his sight king and slave, prince and peasant, are the same, judged only by their devotion or indifference towards him.

David knew that it was God who had made him what he was. Therefore, was he more in God's sight than the lowest of the Israelites? David did not rejoice merely from individual gratitude. It was the purest joy to a heart like David's that to him the blessed privilege was granted of bringing the ark to his city; a proof, indeed, that the Lord deigned to bless Hebron with His immediate presence, and thus it was a time not for individual but for national rejoicing.

Michael does not appear to have been a very religious woman. In no part of her history do we see the workings of piety or religious devotion. Her love for David would seem to have been excited by his lordly qualities, his beauty, and his brave carriage. Had she been a religious woman her joy at the ark's being brought to Hebron would have snuffed out all petty complaints of station or of rank. That she was more attracted to David's brilliant exterior than to his spiritual beauty is clear in this instance, in the scornful contempt with which she regarded him.

David was satisfied with administering a deserved reproof; but God was not. From the punishment which befell Michal we may infer that her sin—the sin of arrogance and scorn for others—was more serious than we might suppose at first glance. At least, the Scriptures make a point of telling us that "Michal the daughter of Saul had no child unto the day of her death." And that was not all.

In the book of Samuel we find mention of a famine in Israel, which proved to David that all the awful actions of Saul and his bloody house were not yet atoned, and reparation to the Gibeonites still to be made. Seven of Saul's nearest descendants they demanded, these Gibeonites, to be delivered up to them, in lieu of either gold or silver, or even execution by the new king. Consequently, David delivered up two of Saul's remaining sons and his five grandsons, who had been borne Adriel by Michal's sister Merab. These grandsons, the Bible tells us, "Michal had brought up for Adriel"; that is, she had adopted them. Thus was Michal doubly childless, and yet visited with a mother's bereavement.

The Scriptures pause briefly over this woman in order to highlight certain qualities and defects endemic to the time of the monarchy. On the one hand, Michal is painted as having the courage to love David, and her love was no ordinary affection. In the face of tyranny and persecution, Michal loved David, and saved his life, even at the risk of her own. She suffered outrage at the hands of her father on account of him, and braved many storms before she saw him rise to the throne. Thus, she is represented as possessing devoted and selfless qualities. She is an example of one whose sterling characteristics arise to obstruct tyranny.

On the other hand, we are not allowed to forget that she was Saul's daughter, a princess. Thus, her scorn is seen as deriving from snobbery, and the effect of such scorn was an affront to God. This affront was directly related to the state of the Jewish people during the monarchy. For the equality underlying the Mosaic law had been threatened by Saul's regency; indeed, the very growth of a royal class bespoke a lessening of those egalitarian sentiments which Moses espoused. The people, even under as great a king as David, who showed by his piety that all creatures were one with God, could not escape the hard fact that they were now ruled over, and that at least temporally they were subject to a specific house, not through love, as they had been under the patriarchs, but through duty. With David as king, of course this was not a burdensome duty, for the man was universally revered. But under a king like Saul it is evident that the Hebrews had abdicated something of their own free will, and come to be slaves to a defective agent of their God.

It was inevitable, then that the arrogance of Michal should arise. In her, the Scriptures symbolize the profound class differences which had formed during the monarchy. Her contempt for David burst from Michal as a natural response, for her class had developed contempt for those born outside the closed circle of the regency. The juxtaposition of her contempt for David's simplicity in the matter of the ark points up the contradictions which were evolving among the Israelites. In an attempt to show the moral condemnation due to class pride, the Scriptures tell the story of Michal in the typically straightforward biblical manner, offsetting Michal's snobbery with David's piety, in order to indicate the deep threat to Mosaic law that the monarchy, in and of itself, represented. For the devotion of David—enlightened king though he was—could not forestall the development of a closed royal class during the period of the monarchy.

Often it is overlooked that the Old Testament, in its dazzling religious and moral grandeur, is also a book of deep political import. The historical evolution of the Jewish people, from nomadic tent-dwellers to a more or less settled farming nation, and then to city-dwellers, is reflected in the Bible; moreover, their political relations are also detailed. In the wanderings of Abraham, for instance, we see that the sociopolitical system was based upon divine revelation, a definite moral order, and custom. Abraham and Sarah, though royalty in the fashion of nomadic tribes, were wont, we have seen, to greet visitors of whatever station with hospitality and an open heart. In Hagar's presence, of course, we notice the customary existence of household slaves, but that slaves were not despised for their *rank* is shown in the ascendancy of Hagar herself to the position of the patriarch's wife. Furthermore, we observe that, during the Captivity, the oppressed and unsettled state of the people required strong leadership: and in Moses' law the need for individual and national responsibility is implicit, with a strong egalitarian tenor to the legal intentions, so as to chasten those tendencies towards idolatry and divisiveness which the people, even as he was given the law, were practicing. And the high position of the judges, of course, was caused by a period of shattering wars and fragmentation: Deborah, even in helping her nation, had to be on guard lest her own general should worship her, at the expense of his own individual responsibility. In the actions of Samson towards Delilah, we see that judge violating his people's cause and slavishly worshiping the flesh of a woman he had taken from the Philistines, thereby setting at naught the Mosaic provisions with regard to women and the efficacy of his own faith. Yet, weak as Samson was, he was looked upon as a leader by his people; we can therefore see how desperately low the people's own faith and responsibility had fallen. It was predictable, then, that the monarchy should arise, for throughout their history the Israelites had displayed but sporadic intentions in the matter of governing themselves in the honest, egalitarian manner envisioned by Moses. Constantly the people were setting leaders above themselves, and even in Moses' time the tragedy of Elisheba points up the virulence with which the members of the leader class could disdain those who had elevated them. Moses was plagued by the inability of his people to govern themselves with fairness, with faith, and with love. But the Old

Testament, by recounting the punishment delivered to those who abdicated their responsibilities, or to those who misused the power given them, makes clear that, in God's eyes, the necessity for a personal and national responsibility was absolutely requisite. Surely this is the case with mankind even now, and here the Old Testament makes a timeless political point.

How far we are from the simple nobility of heart shown by Abraham and Sarah, when we arrive at Michal's contemptuous gaze out of her royal chambers. The esteem of the people for the leadership of Israel had been renewed by David's ascendancy, but the scorn for the people which Saul had displayed was still to be found in his daughter, and, by implication, in the royal household.

Although the people might be chastened by God for their slack disregard of their responsibilities, so were the leaders, too, punished for an unwonted sense of their own rank. We saw that Elisheba's sons were struck down before the very portals of the tabernacle for a crime not greatly different from Michal's. Only because Michal had been a heroine in David's cause does she seem to have escaped a like fate. Even so, in a nation where children were so highly desired, her own punishment was severe.

Politically, then, certain principles begin to emerge in the Old Testament narrative. First, we have the innate nobility of Abraham and Sarah, who ruled by worth and by love; then Moses, who led his people by the greatness of his devotion; then the dark days of the judges, when the leadership wavered from the strength and intelligence of Deborah to the sensual mindlessness of Samson; and then the despotism of Saul. By God's actions in these different epochs, we see the intent of the Old Testament with regard to political power. Where it springs from sincere love of men and faith in God, political power is conceived to be a natural function of the person possessing such merits; but the use of that power must be a function as well of his or her good character. But when power falls into the hands of a tyrant, like Saul, the Old Testament makes it clear that kingship, in itself, is meaningless. A truly democratic spirit who embodies the Mosaic law will not wield power over others but inspire others in the nation's good.

That Moses felt it necessary to impose strictures insuring the equality of the people, regardless of station, sex, or rank, shows the tendency of men to become instruments of oppression. It was not as it had been under a simpler social order, as in Abraham's day, but the darkening portents of a more complex and highly stratified society were visible on the horizon. Moses felt that it was necessary to codify those God-given sentiments which we recognize today as democratic. Under a monarchy, of course, such laws as those Moses promulgated could not have fared very well, in any case. It took the simplicity of a David to remind not only his wife, but his people as well that men were not viewed by their God as on an arbitrary hierarchy.

Michal, therefore, utters her reproach to David against a background of growing and fearful divisiveness in the Hebrew social order. By telling her story, the Old Testament warns against an already accomplished attitude, that of class pride and scorn for the lowly. In the city of Hebron, unlike the rural areas, where the poor and the stranger might glean the harvest of the wealthier Israelites—as we have heard it so touchingly told in Ruth's story—there was no provision against the growth of class oppression. This oppression is more significant, then, than that displayed by Elisheba's sons, who were overproud of their lineage. What Michal symbolizes in this tale is a *social tendency* leading the Israelites away from the moral order that had sanctified their history. It is not insignificant, then, that this strong and courageous woman uttered words that made a mockery of the very love that had once inspired her. For we see in her the paradox and contradiction at work in Jewish society itself during the monarchy.

The Witch of Endor

The monarchy was quite as subject to the influences of idolatry and superstition as had been the period of the judges. This was especially so during Saul's reign. Indeed, his traffic with a witch is a prime example of the bad faith of the king, and indicates the depths to which the Israelites fell during his tyranny.

Now, a witch is seen as the obverse of a prophetess in the Old Testament. Deborah displayed those divine attributes of virtue which drew her near the will and intent of God. Her prophecies and her guidance were from God, the true source of knowledge, and she was the medium by whom the will of the Lord and the puzzling path of duty were made plain to others. A witch, on the other hand, was one who sought knowledge of the future through all the magical charms, incantations, and ceremonies by which the spirits of the dead were sought for interference in the affairs of men; hers was the dark divinity of superstition. The sin of seeking out this sort of woman lay in the fact that one turned from God and sought the base ministrations born of idolatrous religion.

Indeed, witchcraft was a capital offense under Moses' law. He had explicitly told his people that their God was "nigh unto them for all they should call upon Him for." We have seen time and again throughout these biographies that women as well as men could seek the ear of the Lord in prayer. Miriam, Deborah, and Hannah turned to God, not to the dead nor to potions and spells, for assistance and guidance in their times of need. The efficacy of individual prayer we saw illustrated in Hannah's tale; and in Deborah's biography we saw divine knowledge informing the acts of a single remarkable woman. What need, then, had the Israelites of witches? It is a mark of Saul's crude nature that he turned to such a female, and in this female we see the breaking of the law which all too often scarred the monarchy.

It is instructive to quote the story in full, both for its poetic depth and for its vivid force:

Now Samuel was dead, and all Israel had lamented him, and buried him in Ramah, even in his own city. And Saul had put away those that had familiar spirits, and the wizards, out of the land. And the Philistines gathered themselves together, and came and pitched in Gilboa. And when Saul saw the host of the Philistines, he was afraid, and his heart greatly trembled. And when Saul inquired of the Lord, the Lord answered him not, neither by dreams, . . . nor by prophets. Then said Saul unto his servants, Seek me a woman that hath a familiar spirit, that I may go to her, and inquire of her. And his servants said to him, Behold, there is a woman that hath a familiar spirit at Endor. And Saul disguised himself, and put on other raiment, and he went, and two men with him, and they came to the woman by night: and he said, I pray thee, divine unto me by the familiar spirit, and bring me him up whom I shall name unto thee. And the woman said unto him, Behold, thou knowest what Saul hath done, how he hath cut off those that have familiar spirits, and the wizards, out of the land: wherefore then layest thou a snare for my life, to cause me to die? And Saul sware to her by the Lord, saying, As the Lord liveth, there shall no punishment happen to thee for this thing. Then said the woman, Whom shall I bring up unto thee? And he said, Bring me up Samuel. And when the woman saw Samuel, she cried with a loud voice: and the woman spake to Saul, saying, why hast thou deceived me? for thou art Saul. And the king said unto her, Be not afraid; for what sawest thou? And the woman said unto Saul, I saw gods ascending out of the earth. And he said unto her, What for is he of? And she said, An old man cometh up; and he is covered with a mantle. And Saul perceived that it was Samuel, and he stooped with his face to the ground, and bowed himself. And Samuel said to Saul, Why hast thou disquieted me, to bring me up? And saul answered, I am sore distressed; for the Philistines make war against me, and God is departed from me, and answereth me no more, neither by prophets, nor by dreams: therefore I have called thee, that thou mayest make known unto me what I shall do.

Then said Samuel, Wherefore then dost thou ask of me, seeing the Lord is departed from thee, and is become thine enemy? And the Lord hath done to him, as He spake by me: for the Lord hath rent the kingdom out of thine hand, and given it to thy neighbor, even to David: Because thou obeyedst not the voice of the Lord, nor executedst His fierce wrath upon Amalek, therefore hath the Lord done this thing unto thee this day. Moreover the Lord will also deliver Israel with thee into the hand of the Philistines: and to-morrow shalt thou and thy sons be with me: the Lord also shall deliver the host of Israel into the hand of the Philistines.

Then Saul fell straightway all along the earth, and was sore afraid, because of the words of Samuel: and there was no strength in him; for he had eaten no bread all day, nor all the night. And the woman came unto Saul, and saw that he was sore troubled, and said unto him, Behold, thine handmaid hath hearkened unto thy words which thou spakest unto me: now therefore, I pray thee, hearken thou also unto the voice of thine handmaid, and let me set a morsel of bread before thee; and eat, that thou mayest have strength, when thou goest on thy way. But he refused, and said, I will not eat. But his servants, together with the woman, compelled him, and he hearkened unto their voice. So he arose from the earth, and sat upon the bed. And the woman had a fat calf in the house, and she hasted, and killed it, and took flour, and kneaded it, and did bake unleavened bread thereof. And she brought it before Saul, and before his servants; and they did eat. Then they rose up, and went away that night.

We find here not only the source of much of David's later travails, but a complete rejection of God, whose solace in the needs and sorrows of life He had promised the Israelites. Moses' instruction had been that there was no divine anger that might not be placated by sincere repentance; but Saul broke with God and did not repent, even after Samuel announced the Lord's wrath and he lay helpless in the hands of a witch, with all lawful recourse to knowledge and guidance closed to him. He was like an infant, to be cajoled and prodded in his blind sin.

The woman herself seems not to have been of a particularly wicked visage; rather, she was kindly in her actions towards Saul, and was simply turning a penny in her "professional" capacity. She was sincerely afraid when she found herself the medium for a netherworld convocation of kings, but afraid only for her own life, not for her soul or her character. She tried to soften Saul by making him food, in order not to have his fear and resultant wrath fall on her head. She was a witch, much used to employing her sorcery and wiles on dull men.

Abigail

During that period when David was cast out and in fear of extermination by Saul's henchmen, as we have read in Michal's biography, he took for himself another wife. In this woman, Abigail, we see nothing of Michal's princely arrogance, but a great deal, and more, of her courage. In Abigail the Old Testament paints a portrait of surpassing grace and loveliness, intelligence and devotion. The story of their love is set in the tumultuous period of tyranny which Saul's monarchy engendered, and it forms a veritable jewel of serene and abiding affection in the midst of violent treachery.

Even as a wanderer, David's personal qualities of strength and forthrightness drew men to his cause, and he soon became the leader of a small army. David's gallant, generous nature bound these men to him in the fealty of love, as they coursed through the mountain reaches of Israel.

At one point, they encamped in the region of Paran, near the pastures of Carmel, where the high plains were covered with the herds of the cruel and prosperous landowner, Nabel.

Abigail was, at this time, wife of that landowner. The Old Testament attributes only churlishness to Nabal, but to his wife the Scriptures pay her a compliment: "She was a woman of good understanding and of a beautiful countenance." We may speculate, given the divergent natures of these two, that it was an arranged marriage, the prosperity of the man having induced the father of the woman to give her in matrimony. Still, the husband's sour nature seems not to have spoiled the wife's temper, and she remained devoted to him, if aloof from his mean and calculating disposition.

When David and his band of men appeared on the scene, it was sheep-shearing time. Feasting and festival usually attended this operation. It being a dangerous age, however, the workers of the field felt well protected by David's small and vigilant army, and went about the joyous seasonal occupations with special security. David, of course, did not want to appropriate any part of Nabal's flocks, though he was sorely pressed by hunger and privation; thus he waited until the sheep-shearing was done, when men's hearts were more open to their poorer brethren. He sent messengers to the landowner, bidding them greet him in his (David's) name, courteously tender his respects, and ask for the food and drink he and his men so sorely needed. The request is beautifully phrased and shows well the gentility and courtesy that were hallmarks of David's character:

Peace be both to thee and peace be to thine house, and peace unto all that thou hast. And now I have heard that thou hast shearers: now thy shepherds which were with us, we hurt them not, neither was there aught missing unto them, all the while they were in Carmel. Ask thy young men, and they will show thee. Wherefore let the young men find favor in thine eyes: for we come in a good day: give, I pray thee, whatsoever cometh to thine hand unto thy servants, and to thy son David.

There could be no more respectful address than this, and one would expect an equally gracious reply. But Nabal, true to his close-fisted and cruel nature, refused this request in a peremptory manner, and scornfully demanded, "Who is David? and who is the son of Jesse? there be many servants nowadays that break away every man fron his master. Shall I then take my bread, and my water, and my flesh, that I have killed for my shearers, and give it unto men whom I know not whence they be?"

Now, his own shearers could have told him of David's probity in the sheep shearing; but of course he did not ask; he simply followed the dictates of his own ill nature. David had not only restrained his starving men from taking part of Nabal's flocks, but had actually set them to protecting the operation from the marauding bands common in the mountain districts.

David's indignation, when he received this rebuff, was boundless. Though a pious and essentially gentle man, he was also a warrior and a man—a mortal, and subject to fits of anger, like all mortals. He was angered not only by this ill return for his humble and courteous request, but by the return of evil for good. He commanded his men to put on their swords and armament, and marched with them towards Nabal's dwelling, resolved to lay waste to all that belonged to Nabal, and humble him, and crush him. We have no reason to believe that he would not have done so, for he was a fierce warrior, for all his grace and minstrel's gentleness. Warm affection and hot passion coexisted in this man, and he had known, in his wanderings, too much privation not to be mortally offended by a lack of generosity in others. His heated feelings might have carried him to bloody extremes indeed had not the intelligence and nobility of Nabal's wife stopped him.

We see from the events which followed Nabal's rebuff of David the high esteem in which Abigail was held by the household. For instead of attempting to soften the impervious cruelty of Nabal, the shearers sent a message to his wife, knowing full well the generosity and wisdom of the woman.

"Behold," they told her, "David sent messengers out of the wilderness to salute our master; and he railed on them. But the men were very good unto us, and we were not hurt, neither missed we anything, as long as we were conversant with them in the fields: they were a wall unto us both by night and by day, all the while we were with them keeping the sheep. Now therefore know and consider what thou wilt do; for evil is determined against our master, and against all his household; for he is such a man of Belial, that a man cannot speak to him."

From these words we suppose that the shearers had seen enough of David, when in the wilderness together, to have been assured that such ungraciousness would be severely punished. And we may conjecture, too, that their devotion was not so much with Nabal as with his household, and that, no doubt, for Abigail's sake.

Abigail lost no time in responding. Her quick wits and immediate judgment in this matter set her off totally from her husband, who courted disaster for the sake of his own material wealth. Abigail did not consult nor seek to placate Nabal, for she had neither the time nor the inclination. She asked no advice, demanded no assistance, but required only the willing help of her domestics in carrying out her judicious, if hasty, plans. She had, then, not only intelligence, but instincts different from those of her husband, instincts towards good and towards right action. The biblical account of her behavior bears these qualities out:

> Then Abigail made haste, and took two hundred loaves, and two bottles of wine, and five sheep ready dressed, and five measures of parched corn, and an hundred clusters of raisins, and two hundred cakes of figs, and laid them upon asses. And she said to her servants, Go on before me; and she told not her husband Nabal. And it was so as she rode upon the ass that she came down by the covert of the hill, and behold, David and his men came down against her, and she met them. And when Abigail saw David, she hasted and lighted off the ass, and fell before David, and bowed herself to the ground, and fell at his feet and said, Upon me, my lord, upon me let this iniquity be, and let thy handmaid, I pray thee, speak in thine audience, and hear the words of thy handmaid. Let not my lord, I pray thee, regard this man of Belial, even Nabal, for as his name is so is he, Nabal is his name, and folly is with him; but I, thine handmaid, saw not the young men of my lord whom thou didst send. Now therefore, my lord, as the Lord liveth, and as thy soul liveth, seeing the Lord hath withholden thee from coming to shed blood, and avenging thyself with thine own hand, now let thine enemies and they that seek evil to my lord be as Nabal. And now this present that I have brought, let it be given to the

men that follow my lord. I pray thee, forgive the trespass of thine handmaid, and the Lord will certainly make my lord a sure house, because my lord fighteth the battles of the Lord, and evil hath not been found in thee all thy days. Yet a man is risen to pursue thee, and to seek thy soul; but the soul of my lord shall be bound in the bundle of life with the Lord thy God, and the souls of thine enemies them shall He sling out as out of the middle of a sling. And it shall come to pass, when the Lord shall have done to my lord according to all the good that He hath spoken concerning thee, and shall have thee appointed thee ruler over Israel, that this shall be no grief unto thee, nor offense of heart unto my lord, either that thou hast shed blood causeless, or that my lord hath avenged himself; but when the Lord shall have dealt well with my lord, then remember thine handmaid.

A more dignified and tactful address than this could hardly be imagined. She did not flatter the man, but attributed to God his goodness. She deflected his anger by appearing to take the blame upon herself, and strove to lessen the offenses of Nabal by attributing his actions not to malice but to folly, which set him somewhat beneath David's regard.

It was a singularly noble action on Abigail's part to take upon herself the trespass and offer to bear the penalty upon her own shoulders. The evil temperament of Nabal must not only have curtailed all her affection for him, but must repeatedly have exposed her to the cruelty of a surly husband. Yet she thought nothing of these things, and only remembered that, as her husband, he deserved the effort she was making. Neither did she romanticize or seek to cloak the man's nature.

Unselfishness of this sort David could eaily appreciate; his own more gentle side came to the fore when Abigail's words were spoken. His wrath literally vanished before her honorable example.

And David said to Abigail, Blessed be the Lord God of Israel, which sent thee this day to meet me; and blessed be thy advice, and blessed be thou, which hast kept me this day from coming to shed blood, and from avenging myself with mine own hand. For in very deed, as the Lord God of Israel liveth, which hath kept me back from hurting thee, except thou hadst hasted and come to meet me, surely by the morning light there had not been one left to Nabal.

David, then, saw that Abigail had turned him away from committing a great sin; indeed, only he knew how close he had come to venting his anger in outrage—an outrage that, as Abigail pointed out, was more befitting her husband than the great David.

So David received of her hand that which she had brought him, and said unto her, Go up in peace to thine house; see, I have hearkened to thy voice, and have accepted thy person. And Abigail came to Nabal; and behold, he held a feast in his house like the feast of a king; and Nabal's heart was merry within him, for he was very drunken; wherefore she told him nothing, less or more, until the morning light. But it came to pass in the morning, when the wine was gone out of Nabal, and his wife had told him these things, that his heart died within him, and he became as a stone. And it came to pass about ten days after, that the Lord smote Nabal, that he died.

Wisely, then, Abigail had left her husband undisturbed in his inebriated state until the dawn. For she knew him well, and would not trifle with his drunken ways. And in the bleak light of morning she went to him, told him what she had done, and "his heart died within him"—he who had begrudged even the smallest particle of his vast stores was dumbstruck when he realized the disaster he had so narrowly escaped. All the wealth of which he was so jealous would, he saw that morning, have availed him nothing; the young warrior he had slighted as a bootless vagabond with a pack of thieves would have laid everything he owned to waste and destruction. It was the realization of his own petty sins as stacked against a great judgment—and "the Lord smote Nabal."

And when David heard that Nabal was dead, he said, Blessed be the Lord, that hath pleaded the cause of my reproach from the hand of Nabal, and hath kept His servant from evil; for the Lord hath returned the wickedness of Nabal upon his own head. And David sent and communed with Abigail, to take her to him to wife. And when the servants of David were come to Abigail, to Carmel, they spake unto her, saying David sent us unto thee, to take thee to him to wife. And she arose, and bowed herself on her face to the earth, and said, Behold, let thine handmaid be a servant to wash the feet of the servants of my lord. And Abigail hasted, and arose, and rode upon an ass, with five damsels of hers that went after her; and she went after the messengers of David, and became his wife.

We see here that David, upon Nabal's death, was wholly aware of the sin from which Abigail had saved him, and that the nature of that near sin was the doing of what it was only in God's power to do. Abigail had "kept His servant from evil," for she was God's envoy to him in this affair.

And so struck had David been by Abigail's honorable nature, by her courage and right action—not to mention her beauty, for we must not forget that David was a young man, and romantic—that he found it his turn to plead with the woman who had only lately knelt before him as a supplicant.

When Abigail was the petitioner, she used no expression indicative of servility; she sought David's good sense and moral judgment, not his pity. But when she found herself petitioned on behalf of David, she also did the appropriate thing, by showing herself humble before his honest request, and offering to wash the feet of his servants. She seems to have been a woman of "good understanding" indeed, a woman who intuited directly the most fitting response to the world about her. We may easily infer that this woman was a personage of some culture and insight, for she had the intelligence and instincts of a diplomat and the extraordinary grace of a princess. She presented her love in quite as honest a manner as her entreaty.

Now, in worldly station and earthly possessions, David could not compare with Abigail's late husband. He was indeed destined to the kingdom, and Abigail had divined that fact; but there was certainly, at this point, no assurance of that eventuality occurring very soon. David was the chosen of the Lord, and Abigail did not doubt it, but the fact is she traded her wealth, security, and luxury for a life of anxious wandering, continually exposed to danger by Saul and his cutthroats, and to captivity by the neighboring nations. Still, the love and sympathy of David's nature attracted her far more than all her stores, flocks, servants, and comforts. For he offered her a happiness she had never known as the wife of a crude, cruel, malicious miser. Thus was her humility inspired. She recognized in David's request the honest affection of the Lord's own anointed, and no longer considered material comforts of any importance.

And in her new life she did not complain, but was thankful for her first taste of unstinting love. A young woman, given to a churlish man to wed in her youth, forever, it seemed, cut off from the warmth of a kindred nature, Abigail rejoiced in the face of danger. David was a dashing and handsome young man, a man of generous affection, and what he admired, he loved, and loved fully. The fierceness of the warrior's nature, which rose up in his moments of anger, could be softened by truthful and generous behavior in others, and his poet's nature—always the dominant side of him— would overcome the blind anger. Abigail knew this, and was thankful that there dwelt within him a passionate affection every bit as strong as his warrior's incorrigible heat.

There is only one more mention of Abigail in the Old Testament narrative, and in the very situation to which the dangers of David's wanderings exposed her.

About two years after his marriage to Abigail, David took refuge in the kingdom of Gath, and obtained from Achish, the king of that land, the town of Ziklag, which, though situated in the territory of Simeon, had till then belonged to the Philistines. In that city David and his followers, with their wives and children, formed a small Hebrew enclave, which was for them both home and refuge. But sometime after David had received the gift of Ziklag the Philistines gathered together all their armies in an attempt to make war on Achish. David's band joined the armies of Achish, but were then marshaled out of the war effort due to the suspicion of the Gathian generals. David and his men were gone about three days on this abortive mission; when they returned to Ziklag they found the city a heap of smoking ruins, and their wives and children all carried off. The Amalekites had invaded the town during their absence, had burnt the ground behind them, and had abducted every single woman and child in the enclave. "Then David and the people that were with him lifted up their voices and wept, until they had no more power to weep."

David mourned not only the loss of his beautiful Abigail, but was "greatly distressed for the people spake of stoning him, because the soul of all the people was grieved, every man for his sons and for his daughters." True to his deeply religious nature, especially in times of trouble, David "encouraged himself in the Lord his God," and made prayerful inquiry. And God answered him, bidding him to make pursuit of the Amalekites: "For thou shalt surely overtake them, and without fail recover all."

Suffice it to say that David did indeed recover Abigail and all his kind on the expedition: "There was nothing lacking to him, neither small nor great, neither sons nor daughters, nor anything they [the Amalekites] had taken to them; David recovered all."

Enough has been revealed of Abigail's character to surmise what her conduct must have been during this trying time. She saw the city of her husband burnt and sacked and her and all her female companions, with their helpless children, carried off by lawless men. She was exposed to every sort of horror. A wild attack, a hurried flight, and then the agony of captivity. She thought David and his men with Achish on a lengthy campaign, their return distant and uncertain. Then the sudden descent of David and his men, the awful strife, lasting all of one night and into the next, and the final, bloody victory of her husband. We are given strong evidence of the fortitude and calm patience of Abigail and the Israelite captives.

Abigail was, to be sure, a woman of "good understanding"—in rabbinical literature, indeed, she is listed as one of the prophetesses, along with Sarah, Miriam, Deborah, Hannah, Huldah, and Esther. We have already noted the little influence which Nabal's mean temper had upon Abigail's character. From her wise forbearance of him, both in acting without his knowledge in seeking David, and in not mentioning the effect of that interview until he was in a state to hear it, we can easily infer that she not only bore with his cruel disposition, but well knew how to manage it—not an easy task, and one which only the most circumspect intelligence can attempt. Neither do we find her displaying triumph at her own skill in turning wrath aside. That she had been permitted to save her household from imminent danger was enough for her; and if God had not ruled otherwise, she would have returned to all her usual duties.

We learn of Abigail's constant superiority of judgment by the fact that her servants went to her without hesitation. They must have frequently confided in her judgment before, or else they could not have demonstrated such implicit trust in a moment of crisis.

Abigail's profound influence on David is clearly evident in the success of her appeal; quick judgment and a few well-chosen words saved her and her household from destruction, and David from committing a grave sin.

She must have had a good knowledge of human nature to have so soon turned aside David's wrath. Discernment, intellect, and poetic talent all breathe in her eloquent appeal, and evince an elevation of remarkable intelligence. She had, like Miriam and Hannah, a knack for the beautiful and penetrating phrase, and understood intuitively the rhythm of proud and earnest entreaty.

This poetic faculty—so much a part of the natures of the great women of Israel—is emblematic of a cultured sensibility, a sensibility we must surmise she nurtured all on her own, for Nabal's intelligence is in no way alluded to. Indeed, the man's actions were brutish in every respect, and except for his great wealth, he could lay no claim to distinction of any kind. What Abigail possessed was her own, acquired by her own efforts.

Her nature sprang, also, from a correct understanding of duty—duty to her first husband, though he was in the wrong, and duty to God and man. She showed amazing percipience in regard to Nabal's shortcomings, and immediate apprehension of David's virtues, even in the throes of his blind rage. The Old Testament portrays here a woman of remarkable temperament, whose intelligence and emotions were in perfect balance.

This balanced character stood Abigail in good stead during the sacking of Ziklag and in her subsequent captivity. As the wife of the future king, the other women must naturally have turned to her for guidance, and their generally steadfast and pious courage must have been in no small part due to Abigail's influence.

With Michal, David was to be at odds, but with Abigail he found that perfect fusion of careful reflection, generosity, and poetic talent which he so greatly appreciated in others and cultivated in himself. The Old Testament tells us how quick he was to discern the woman's extraordinary qualities. Himself a poet, and a good and generous man, he could not have done better than take this woman as his wife; indeed, his tendency towards unthinking anger was offset by Abigail's more careful and diplomatic nature. Little wonder, then, that he should bewail her capture by the Amalekites, for in losing her he lost not only a beautiful woman and a dutiful wife, but an intellect equal to his own, and a companion who loved what he loved, and gave what he gave. The reader's joy is indeed great, therefore, when he hears that "David recovered all."

—*The Woman of Tekoah*—

During David's reign, the most heart-rending situation occurred when the king's own son, Absalom, rebelled against his father. Absalom was always David's favorite, and, even upon the death of that treacherous offspring, the good king expressed the wish that he had rather been the one who had died. Probably no greater love has been given son by father than what which David gave Absalom. And no love, certainly, has been more senselessly spurned.

During the course of this sad sequence of events, which so afflicted David, Joab, David's general, sought to intercede with the king on Absalom's behalf. He cast about for a method, and finally hit upon the use of a "wise woman," who, in this brief episode with which we are dealing, epitomized the high and respected station of women under the Mosaic law and in Israelite society. The woman of Tekoah was sent to David to soften the king's heart towards the exiled Absalom, and she showed the great intellectual insight in her attempt.

The woman of Tekoah related to David that she was a widow who had two sons, one of whom, while arguing with the other, had smitten and slain him. The whole family had risen against the widow, commanding her to deliver up the survivor, that they might revenge his brother's death by also killing him. They intended, said the woman, to "quench my coal which is left, and not leave my husband neither name nor remainder upon the earth."

David desired her to return to her home in peace; he said that he would deliver a judgment concerning her. The woman lingered, however, and he said, "Whosoever saith aught unto thee, bring him unto me, and he shall not touch thee any more."

> Then said she, I pray thee, let the king remember the Lord thy God, that thou wouldst not suffer the revengers of blood to destroy any more, lest they destroy my son. And he said, As the Lord liveth, there shall not one hair of thy son fall to the ground.

From this exchange we deduce that the crime of the one brother against the other came under the accidental murders, where, according to the law, the slayer was permitted to seek the cities of refuge. It was, of course, a fictitious tale which the woman of Tekoah told David; she had been charged by Joab with the task of softening him. The means she chose to do so were almost on the level of parable, and showed, in the symbolic manner of parable, a strict grasp of the law. The woman asserted that she was a widow, and consequently the particular care of her brethren. Her position was sanctified, and therefore David not only heard her plea, and promised that he would take her in charge, but pledged himself to an even greater leniency than the law allowed. In his own case, vis-à-vis Absalom, a case exactly similar, David had done such violence to his own parental feelings that three years had elapsed since he had looked on his favorite son, towards whom the Scripture relates "his soul longed to go forth."

David was a respecter of God's word, more in his own case then in others'. The laws of his country might not be transgressed, or stretched, or softened, though he was the sovereign. And yet for a mourning widow his kind heart melted, and the law accordingly blurred. We see, then, that women in Israel were far from being slighted or less regarded than men. On the contrary, the king's son was to languish in exile, whereas the widow's son was to be protected and pardoned.

The woman of Tekoah divined these contradictions in David's rich nature. She stood firmly upon what she knew to be the special position of a bereaved woman in Israel, in making her symbolic plea, and later her argument on behalf of Absalom, to David. She chose the most piercing of intellectual examples in order to bring out the contradictory character of David's actions, and to reveal to him, even before she had made her argument, the possible alternatives to his own parental dilemma.

Not satisfied with the favor granted the supposed widow, the woman of Tekoah proceeded to entreat the king: "Let thine handmaid speak, I pray thee, one word unto my lord the king. And the king said, Say on." Boldly, unhesitatingly, the woman turned reprover of her sovereign, and making her own case the king's, pronounced it a faulty judgment, or else he would long since have called home his own banished son.

The appeal was judicious and the logic impeccable. There was a seriousness in her appeal that bespoke a high degree of education in the subject of the law. Indeed, throughout these biographies of Hebrew women we have seen, not once or twice, but many times, the high level of mentality of the women in general in Israel. It was nothing unusual that women such as this one of Tekoah were turned to; for wisdom and its acquisition was not, in law and in fact, the province of Hebrew men only.

After her appeal and argument, David intuited the manipulations of his general, and addressed the woman of Tekoah as his equal—instead of demanding the truth, as was his royal prerogative: "Hide not from me, I pray thee, the thing that I shall ask thee. And the woman said, let my lord the king now speak. And the king said, Is not the hand of Joab with thee in all this?" The whole matter was consequently exposed; but no anger at the deception followed. The king's word had passed, and though judgement had been made on a fictitious case, he saw its symbolic importance, and he would not withdraw it. The young man Absalom was recalled from his place of exile and brought by Joab to Jerusalem.

Still, true to his own harsh judgments where his own feelings were concerned, David did not see Absalom for fully two years, though they resided in the same town. Now, had the woman of Tekoah's story been true, David would have allowed her the blessing of her son's continued presence and the balm of full pardon.

The incident is important to the understanding of the position of women in Israel. By Joab's seeking a woman to bring the king around to a more reasonable view; by the scant difficulty she encountered in obtaining a hearing in the royal chambers; by the kindness and sentiment which dictated the monarch's manner and words towards her—by all these indications we see the strong, solid status women commanded, even in days as difficult as those of the monarchy. To be sure, women were, we see in this account, more highly thought of then they are in most modern nations, for even warriors and courtiers did not disapprove of using the woman of Tekoah's aid, and a king himself followed her advice, not only when she entreated him on her own behalf, but when the tables were turned and she addressed him on his.

Rizpah

There is, regarding the descendants of Saul, a strange, sad tale in which the devotion of a woman, Rizpah, leaves the most indelible impression.

Impious acts were committed by Saul's descendants, for which David smote them, one and all. Only Rizpah, daughter of Aiah, was left to mourn them. Day and night, from the barley harvest until the rainy season, a period of many weeks, Rizpah kept solitary watch beside the mouldering bodies of the last remnants of Saul's bloody house. There are volumes concerning steadfast fidelity to the dead, concerning lingering love for perished loved ones, in the simple verses by which Rizpah's devotion is represented in the Scriptures.

"She took sackcloth and spread it for her upon the rock, and suffered neither the birds of the air to rest upon them [the corpses] by day, nor the beasts of the field by night."

Scorched by the harvest sun by day, chilled with the dew by night, Rizpah watched over her dead, frustrating the vultures and braving the scavenging beasts which lurked everywhere about her. The law was that her household could not be buried, and thus, without complaint or reproach, she remained their single watchful mourner, bestowing the dignity of her devotion on those whom Israel had denied the dignity of burial. Hers was the most simple and patient of virtues, and admiration for her was widespread.

Indeed, word of her courage and fidelity reached David, and his heart softened towards the house of his predecessor, in spite of the impieties which had been committed. Thus he ordered that the bones of Saul and of Jonathan, and of those that were there with Rizpah, be buried with due honor in the land of Saul's tribe. And thus it was that the fearful ignominy of denying burial to the dead was removed from Saul's descendants through the devotion of a woman.

———*The Woman of Abel*———

After the death of Absalom, more troubles beset the kingdom of David. And out of these troubles arose a situation potentially as disastrous as the rebellion of David's favorite son. But a brave and patriotic woman strode forth into the fray and proved the tremendous power women could wield, and the great peacemaking influence they could exert.

A quarrel took place, upon Absalom's death, between the men of Israel and the tribe of Judah, as to who should have the greater influence over David. "And the words of the men of Judah were fiercer than the words of the men of Israel," in consequence of which a man called Sheba blew a trumpet and proclaimed, "We have no part in David; neither have we inheritance in the son of Jesse; every man to his tents, O Israel"—the war cry of the Jews. "So every man of Israel went up from David, and followed Sheba, the son of Bichri; but the men of Judah clave unto their king."

A war naturally followed. And Joab with a large army "went from Jerusalem to pursue Sheba." His proclamation, "He that is for David let him go after Joab," recalled the Israelites who had vacillated to Sheba's standard, and Sheba himself, and his remaining army, were compelled to take refuge in the city of Abel. There Joab besieged them, throwing his battering rams against the wall, so that slaughter and destruction seemed inevitable. Indeed, no resistance appeared from within. Not one man had the courage and wisdom to come forward, either to pacify Joab or to meet him in battle. A hesitation no doubt occasioned by the fear of Sheba, the natural reluctance to deliver up those who had taken refuge in their city and the greater fear of rising against David. However, the downfall of the city seemed imminent.

But there was a wise and stouthearted woman within the city walls, who, boldly risking personal danger, both from the army of Joab without and the rage of Sheba and his supporters within, suddenly appeared upon the walls and called aloud, "Hear, hear;

say, I pray thee, unto Joab, Come near hither, that I may speak with thee."

The attack involuntarily ceased, and soldiers and general must have gazed with some astonishment on the vision appearing so bravely before them. Joab approached, and the woman bade him hear her: "Hear the words of thine handmaid. And he said, I do hear. Then she spake, saying, They were wont to speak in old time, saying, They shall surely ask council at Abel, and so they ended the matter"—a reference to the councils held at Abel in former years, councils which had fairly settled matters without bloodshed. Joab's coming upon the city in hostile fashion had, the woman told him, checked the consultation of all who, like herself, were "peaceable and faithful in Israel."

The woman referred to a Mosaic law in this speech.

> When thou comest nigh unto a city to fight against it, then proclaim peace unto it. And it shall be, that all the people that is found therein shall be tributaries unto thee, and they shall serve thee. And if it will make no peace with thee, but will make war against thee, then thou shalt besiege it.

Joab's anger and zeal in the defense of his king seem to have overshadowed this merciful ordinance, leaving the people no choice in their actions. The city was within David's dominions, and the inhabitants his own subjects. The woman expressed this in her concluding words to Joab: "Thou seekst to destroy a city and mother in Israel: why wilt thou swallow up the inheritance of the Lord?"

These were bold words, and yet wise ones, too, all the more remarkable in that they were conjured up in the midst of a siege. The woman placated Joab by using the words "listen to thine handmaid," and by then going directly into an appeal to Joab's best and holiest feelings, which could only have emanated from a mind long accustomed to rational and shrewd thought. Her sole plea was also shrewd: that she was a "mother in Israel," a station to which the fiercest and most hard-bitten natures in Israel could never refuse reverence.

Far be it, far be it from me to swallow up or destroy—the matter is not so, but a man of Mount Ephraim, Sheba the son of Bichri by name, hath lifted up his hand against the king, even against David. Deliver him only, and I will depart from the city. And the woman said, Behold, his head shall be thrown to thee over the wall. Then the woman went unto all the people in her wisdom; and they cut off the head of Sheba the son of Bichri, and cast it out to Joab; and he blew a trumpet, and they retired from the city every man to his tent. And Joab returned to Jerusalem and to the king.

Needless to say, it was an act of far greater mercy to demand the head of Sheba than to expose men, women, and children, in countless numbers, to the wrath of the general's cruel sword. The woman's intentions were to save life, not take it, and because her efforts were successful she is accorded wisdom in the Old Testament.

It is unlikely that her wise counsel to her townspeople was an impulse of the moment. Hebrew women must have had a voice in the ruling bodies of their cities; their position must have been elevated. In an unruly state, as Israel was at that time, wisdom was no more uncultivated than it is now. Had there been any law confining women to a particular sphere, prohibiting their interference in religious or political matters, wisdom would have been no more publicly possible than it was privately urged.

One has only to imagine the condition of the beleaguered city to form an idea of the significance of women in those times. A flurry of conflicting opinions as to what should be done, the presence of an arch rebel, the terrors of the siege, the dissolution of all normal order and its replacement by panic—out of this maelstrom came a woman who alone had the foresight and cool courage to make the best of an awful situation, who alone, apparently, had a good enough grasp of tradition and the law to make an efficacious entreaty. Joab would not have listened to simple pleas—his rage was too great. Only the bold vision of this woman, commanding his attention on the walls, could bring him and his men up short; and only an argument steeped in the best traditions of the land could make him listen. The woman of Abel played shrewdly upon his feelings; moreover, she brought his intellect to rule over his anger. Thus, she saved herself and her townspeople with a truly amazing fusion of wit, cunning, penetration, and knowledge. She was a "wise woman" indeed.

The Harlots before Solomon

The term *harlot* is often used in the Old Testament, and it refers to the same kind of woman—a prostitute—that it does today. But as used in the Scriptures it also connotes an innkeeper or hostess, or women of the servile classes outside of established households, who had neither rank nor wealth nor the favor of landowners or royalty. It is in this latter sense that we must understand *harlot* as applied to those women who came before Solomon for that famous judgment.

Although of the servile classes, these women, we read, were the first to gain access to Solomon upon his ascension to the throne. It was not that there were no lower courts available under Mosaic law, but if anyone demanded the judgment of the monarch himself, then his or her case was heard, regardless of station.

Surrounded by his officers and servants, in the splendid array which marked all the proceedings of King Solomon, the monarch listened with patient and sympathetic attention to the tale of affliction so boldly spoken before him. It was a sad and twisted tale, and so difficult to judge wisely that the young king was sorely tested, and many who might otherwise have ignored the case, listened attentively to see what their new ruler would decide. The two harlots who stood before him were, in a sense, putting their own sovereign on trial.

These two women lived in the same house, and to each of them a child was born, the one born within three days of the other. They were alone within the house, and the child of the one woman died, and she arose at midnight and changed the dead for the living. When her companion awoke in the morning to nurse the babe, she found it dead, and not the child she had borne. Thus she became the complainant against her housemate.

After the complainant narrated her tale before the king, the other women said that it was not true, saying, "Nay, but the living is my son, and the dead is thy son!" The other said, "No, but the dead is thy son, and the living is my son."

A difficult case, indeed. But Solomon made not the slightest pause. Repeating the charge and the denial, so as to make the circumstances clear to all, he continued, "Bring me a sword." When this was done, he delivered that memorable sentence which revealed his wisdom and has come down to us as the epitome of shrewd insight.

"Divide the living child in two, give half to the one, and half to the other."

A seemingly mad judgment on the face of it; in fact, however, it was delivered with a tremendous knowledge of human nature. For "then spake the woman whose the living child was unto the king, for her bowels yearned unto her son: Oh, my lord, give her the living child, and in no wise slay it! But the other said, Let it be neither mine nor thine, but divide it! And the king answered and said, Give her [the first speaker] the living child, and in no wise slay it; she is the mother thereof!"

Solomon tested the truth or falsehood of the situation by an appeal to the heart, and decided according to its unguarded manifestation. As a result of the case of these two woman, Solomon's wisdom has become axiomatic.

The case is also an indication that *feelings* were as much a part of Mosaic law as legalisms. The beautiful outburst of the true mother, in giving up her son so as not to see him slain and thus committing perjury, was enough to convince Solomon, who saw the source of justice in the human heart, of the truth.

The Woman of Shunem

There was a "great woman" in the town of Shunem, a woman of rank and consequence, to whose hospitality Elisha often turned when that prophet passed through the district. The benevolent character of this woman marks the heights that women of comfortable station in Israel could attain, placing their all at the disposal of their God.

It was not the custom of the prophets to enter the houses of the great and eat at their luxurious tables, for they preferred the humble meal and lowly house, considering them in accord with their divine mission. It was unusual, then, that Elisha chose to board with the woman of Shunem and her husband. And when Scripture tells us that this woman "constrained him to eat bread," we see his own innate reluctance. And yet, "so it was, that as oft as he passed by, he turned in thither to eat bread," and in so doing, it may be inferred, he found her one of "the seven thousand who had not bowed the knee to Baal nor kissed him," as the time of the prophets was as riven with idolatry as that of the judges. Thus, Elisha accepted the woman's hospitality with the deference of the pious, who recognize in whatever rank the kindred in spirit. His mission of love and devotion to the "one sole invisible God" led him to judge all by their piety and devotion, not by their rank.

Still, he had to be "constrained" to eat at the woman's table, for at first he probably feared that the wealth and luxury which marked the dwelling was infused with the same vice and impiety which degraded the wealthy persons of the land; but the second time he needed no constraint, for one interview was sufficient to prove the spiritual elevation of his hosts, and that they were those with whom God's prophet might enjoy innocence and peace.

Not content with proffering hospitality, the woman of Shunem said to her husband, "Behold now, I know this is a holy man of God, which passeth by us continually. Let us make him a little chamber, I pray thee, in the wall; and let us set for him there a bed, and a table, and a stool, and a candlestick: and it shall be, when he cometh to us, that he shall turn in thither."

Her husband's acquiescence was obtained, and her plan accomplished, and "it fell on a day that he [Elisha] came thither, and he turned into the chamber and slept there." Thus the woman's character is beautifully illustrated. She was eager to show kindness, eager to harmonize her actions and her religious impulses.

She did not at first know that Elisha was a prophet, but simply respected him for his holy ways. Her ignorance in the matter only enhanced the benevolence of her nature. There was nothing in his appearance to mark his special, God-given station, nothing in his simple manner to indicate his extraordinary endowments—nothing, that is, but piety, gentleness, and courtesy. He was a wanderer, with no settled home or occupation. But no doubt the woman came to acknowledge his qualities as beyond what they appeared to be. And she knew that the bustle of a large establishment such as her own was no fit place for a man of prayer and contemplation; even a room to himself within the house would not have permitted him the privacy he required; and so, to remedy this, the woman, with her ready wit, conceived of a chamber expressly for him, with an entrance of its own, furnished to his ascetic tastes.

The place was built and outfitted according to the woman's specifications, and although Elisha said nothing when shown to this chamber, he called, in the morning, for his hostess. She, of course, was of a truly refined and gracious temper, and had not intruded upon him when he arrived. She had wished him to feel the security of a private chamber, made up specially for him; she did *not* wish him to feel an obligation to her. She simply kept in retirement, with the thought that it was in her power to add to the comfort of a man of the Lord. She came to him only when called.

"Behold!" said Elisha to her, "thou hast been careful for us with all this care . . . what is to be done for thee? wouldst thou be spoken for to the king, or to the captain of the host?" And she answered, "I dwell among mine own people."

There is a mild reproof in her reply, that anyone might think she expected reward for her kindness. Her simple statement, "I dwell among mine own people," closed the matter quickly, reflecting her truly generous nature. But Elisha was not satisfied. He no doubt wished to make public that no action taken out of pure love of God and reverence for His ministers should pass without notice; and hearing that her husband was old and that she had no child he spoke to the woman again. And "when he had called her, she stood at the door"—expressing her reluctance to accept any reward, with both humility and dignity in her behavior.

This time, however, no offer of reward embarrassed or offended the good woman. The prophet neither asked nor sought her desires, but at once promised. "Thou shalt embrace a son."

"Nay, my lord," answered the woman, "thou man of God, do not lie unto thine handmaid."

She spoke calmly, as she had previously spoken, but not quite so firmly, seeking to strengthen her faith in the promise with the recollection that this was in truth a man of God, even while she entreated him not to deceive her—the entreaty proving how long she must have yearned for an event such as Elisha promised her.

And it came to pass that the promise was fulfilled, and the woman of Shunem was delivered of a son. Years passed; the woman's time was consumed in the careful rearing of her child. Her love for him was boundless, for she had no doubt resigned herself, before Elisha's promise, to a childless life, which made the blessing of motherhood far more precious to her than to other women. Then an event transpired which, if possible, made her grief greater than that of other women.

The child grew old enough to leave his mother's side, and sometimes he accompanied his father on journeys about the estate. On one of these excursions the boy fell ill, crying, "My head! my head!" Thinking it only a minor complaint, common to children, the father had the boy sent back to his mother: "And when they had taken him and brought him to his mother, he sat on her knees till noon and died."

No wailing escaped the mother's lips; she was as reserved and controlled now as ever.

She rose and went up, and laid him on the bed of the man of God, and shut the door upon him, and went out. And she called to her husband, and said, Send me, I pray thee, one of the young men and one of the asses, that I may run to the man of God and come again. And he said, Wherefore wilt thou go to him today? it is neither new moon, nor Sabbath. And she said, It shall be well.

Even to her husband, then, the woman of Shunem was silent as to their heavy affliction, for she wished not to trouble him until all hope was dead. She took the full burden of grief upon herself, in the courageously self-sustained manner that marked her whole character. She would act before she would weep, seek help before she would mourn; and the great devotion she bore her husband was evident in her judgment in this matter.

"She saddled an ass, and said to her servant, Drive on, and go forward, slack not thy riding for me, except I bid thee." The heat and dust of the journey meant nothing to her; she had but one thought: to reach the man of God. He alone had promised her "a child from the Lord," and only he had the power, by prayer, to restore him to life again.

The way was not so very long; but to the mother it must have seemed an interminable period of time before they reached Mount Carmel. And how did she know the holy one was there? She knew his wandering ways, and that in all probability he would *not* be there. But she followed her instincts, the instincts of faith. Elisha was at Mount Carmel; indeed, he espied her before she saw him, and sent his servant out to meet her. The servant went down and inquired after her well-being and that of her husband and child. She answered him just as she had answered her husband's earlier inquiry: "All is well." For hers was not a grief to be broadcast; it was to be poured into the ear of only one man.

Her magnificent self-control did not desert her until she was shown into the presence of Elisha, at whose feet she sank, powerless. She could only clasp the prophet's knees and gaze on his face in agony, so that Elisha's servant became alarmed. "Let her alone," the holy man reproved him, "for her soul is vexed within her; and the

Lord has hid it from me, and has not told me."

Finally, the woman said, "Did I desire a son of my lord? Did I not say, Do not deceive me?"

The woman of Shunem could not utter the words; she could not say that her child was dead. There is a subtle reproach in her reply: for had she not been given the boy, for whom she had not asked, then she would not have known such grief. But there is faith in her words, also, the faith of one who knows that what comes from God comes with love, a love that might redeem the prophet's promise.

Elisha required no further information; promptly he desired his servant to take his staff and neither loiter nor speak by the way until he had laid it on the face of the child. But the mother insisted: "As the Lord liveth, and as thy soul liveth, I will not leave thee." No one would do but Elisha, and he neither rebuked nor denied her, but rose and followed her.

Restoring the dead was a greater miracle than any Elisha had yet performed; he quickened his steps, and rushed to his own chamber in the woman's house, where the child lay, "and shut the door upon them twain, and prayed unto the Lord."

He might foretell events, might amplify oil, render poison harmless, feed a hundred men with twenty loaves and a few baskets of fruit, make iron swim, and know the thoughts of a king a hundred miles away, but life and death were "of the Lord," and the power for such a thing could only issue from simple prayer.

Time passed; how long it was the suffering mother could not tell. Finally, the prophet's servant bade her enter the chamber; and there, upon the bed, alive, arms outstretched, was her son. "Take up thy son," said Elisha. The prophet's own faith, and the magnanimity of the prophet's God, had brought her son back to life. She sank to the floor in a faint.

When she recovered, she did not speak to Elisha, but simply bowed down before him in silent homage and acknowledgment of his power, clasped her son to her breast, and left the chamber.

This woman's actions are a study in cultured graciousness. Not given to hysterics, nor to panic, she acted out of a faith in God and an understanding of the proper ways to carry herself. She bestowed generosity and kindness on others in such a way as to leave them in their dignity, and sought help herself in a dignified way. Such a harmonious character held her in good stead over the succeeding years, when she became a widow at last.

Throughout these years Elisha never lost sight of the woman of Shunem, and probably continued to occupy the small chamber in her house whenever he passed through the town.

At one point, the prophet foresaw that disaster was about to smite Israel. Thus he advised the removal of the woman of Shunem's household, a removal that must have been very painful to her, whose home had always been in one spot. But she never doubted Elisha.

"Arise," he told her, "and go thou and thine household, and sojourn wheresoever thou canst sojourn: for the Lord hath called for a famine; and it shall also come upon the land seven years." Unhesitatingly, the woman "arose, and did after the saying of the man of God: and she went with her household, and sojourned in the land of the Philistines seven years." It was a hard and faithless land to which she went, but she never once wavered from the advice of the man she trusted with her entire being.

At the end of the seven years, the woman and her household returned to Israel. She found her home and land seized and her crops and dwellings in ruin and privation. With calm self-possession, the woman went herself and made complaint before the king, demanding that he return her house and land to her. She did not seek the assistance of Elisha. She asked no favor for herself, nor any advancement for her son. The heart which once had answered, "I dwell among mine own people," had not changed. As a woman and a widow, her sole plea was the justice of her case.

At the very moment the woman of Shunem came before the king, that monarch was, it so happened, in consultation with one of Elisha's servants, and this servant was reciting the wonders that Elisha had accomplished, among them the restoration of the woman's son.

"Behold, my lord, O king," exclaimed the servant, "this is the woman, and this is her son, whom Elisha restored to life. And when the king asked the woman, she told him."

So strong was the impression made upon the king by her narrative that he turned at once to his officers and said, "Restore all that was hers, and all the fruits of the field, since the day that she left the land, even until now."

Not only, then, were her lands and possessions restored, but they were restored at their full value for the seven years of her absence. Through her exertions she received her rightful due, and her son, his inheritance; and once again the woman's fate was tied intimately to the influence of Elisha and to the will of God.

The special charm of this woman's character is its unity, its harmonious blending of dignity and humility. In every crisis, adversity, or bleak period, in prosperity as well as health, we see her in the same calm and beautiful light. There is an intense undercurrent of strong feeling beneath her reserved surface, which, while it caused her to suffer deeply, also endowed her with the greatest capacity for joy. A cultured sensibility breathed from her every gracious gesture. Her elevated position, her domestic and social influence, convince us that, even in this period of national anarchy for the Hebrews, women were still in possession of all the liberty and privileges granted them by Mosaic law.

It was with no thought of reward that she showed hospitality to Elisha, yet from that one deed all her subsequent happiness sprung. He was the chosen servant of the Lord, and a service done to him was an offering to God. From first to last, the character of the woman of Shunem offers an example of what high station can accomplish when put to the uses of the Lord. Her proper use of wealth and rank, her moderation in all circumstances, her firmness in affliction, her wonderful control of her every emotion, her unselfish endurance of anxiety and anguish, her calm yet energetic prosecution of her and her son's rights are to be pointed to with pride by Israelites, for they reveal the correct conduct of those of wealth and power.

The Maid of Israel

Another of the faithful during Elisha's time was a woman—rather, a girl—of a much different station that that of the woman of Shunem, but her character was no less admirable.

In one of their marauding strikes against the humbled Israel, the Syrians carried off, among their spoils, a little maid. She became the property of Naaman, the captain of the armies of the King of Syria. This Naaman was a man of valor, and had frequently been the cause of Syria's deliverance. He installed the maid of Israel in his household, as one of his wife's handmaids. He himself remained aloof from the occupations of his establishment, and closeted from his household because he had lately contracted leprosy.

It was a hard change for the maid of Israel, to be torn from her home and family and sold into servitude to an idolatrous house. From her later actions, we know that she was a deeply religious girl, one of those who "had not bowed the knee to Baal," for whom Israel was more than a *place.* Her roots were there; moreover, it was the land of her God.

Still, she had a resilient and spritely nature, and quickly gained favor with Naaman's wife. She seemed to have become even somewhat indulged, for she was able to speak freely and without fear, whenever she wanted to communicate with her mistress.

At one point, the maid of Israel, perceiving the hard burden which Naaman's disease had become to her mistress, made a suggestion as simple and direct as her own deep faith in the "one sole invisible God."

> And she said unto her mistress, Would God my lord were with the prophet that is in Samaria! for he would recover him of his leprosy. And one went in and told this lord [Naaman], saying, Thus and thus saith the maid that is of the land of Israel.

Evidently, then, the maid was one of the truly faithful who had either known or seen Elisha, and witnessed his miracles. Her own childish faith is beautifully represented by these few words, for she knew that the Hebrew could find refuge in the love and miraculous power of God.

A peculiar sanctity had always surrounded the Hebrew, in the eyes of other nations. The miraculous deeds of Hebrew history were well known to the Syrians, who, though they held Israel in subjection, still looked upon her with wonder and awe.

Therefore, the maid's suggestion was not so far-fetched to her master's mind as one might think, given that she was but one of his wife's handmaids. And besides, Naaman would doubtless have clutched at any straw, for leprosy was incurable in those times, a disease of slow, hideous wasting away. Certainly it was worth the effort for him to seek out a prophet in the land of Israel, a prophet whose fame had spread even to Syria.

Naaman turned with the maid's story to his monarch, who felt sorely the loss of his captain. This king looked upon Israel's king, Ahab, as his vassal; thus the Syrian king, taken, like Naaman, with the child's account of Elisha, made his captain a splendid caravan with silver and gold and "ten changes of raiment" and a royal letter addressed to Ahab, and sent Naaman into Israel in search of the man of God. In the letter, the Syrian king commanded Ahab to exert his entire influence in bringing about the meeting of Naaman and Elisha.

And so the leprous captain of all-powerful Syria journeyed with his magnificent retinue into the land of his enemies. When he arrived at Ahab's capital and was issued into his presence, the interview was a difficult one, for Ahab raged at what he felt to be an intrusion upon his dignity.

Now, Ahab was not, as we shall see in the biography of Jezebel, on the best of terms with his God, his people, or his prophet, Elisha. When he had read the royal message, he flew into a petulant and ill-mannered fit, proclaiming, "Am I God, to kill and to make alive, that this man doth send unto me to recover a man from his leprosy? See, how he seeketh a quarrel against me!"

Ahab went so far, in his anger, as to rend his own clothes and make ominous—if empty—intimations of aggression against Syria for this "affront" to his kingly dignity. He did not see that the captain of Syria came out of desperation, on the advice of an Israelite maid, whose faith, truth to tell, far outshone that of the sovereign's.

But Elisha knew the true nature of the circumstances. Perhaps he had heard of the pious little maid whose devotion to God had prompted her merciful suggestion, even to her oppressor. And certainly he knew the importance of proving to a powerful Syrian the still greater power of God. For when Elisha heard of the arrival of Naaman, and of the royal interview, he sent to Ahab, saying, "Wherefore hast thou rent thy clothes? Let him [Naaman] come now to me, and he shall know that there is a Prophet in Israel."

Thus the captain, in all his splendor, made his way to Mount Carmel, and drew up before the prophet's door. He sent in his messenger and waited for the prophet's appearance. But Elisha did not appear; indeed, he sent the messenger back with the words, "Go and wash in Jordan seven times, and thy flesh shall come again to thee, and thou shalt be clean."

Naaman saw these words as arrogance—why, the man did not even deign to come to the door! "I thought he would come out to me," raged Naaman, "and stand and call on the name of Jehovah his God, and strike his hand over the place and recover the leper. Are not Abana and Pharpar, river of Damascus, better than all the waters of Israel? may I not wash in them and be clean?" He ordered his caravan about, and left Mount Carmel in a rage.

But his servants prevailed upon Naaman when his anger had cooled, and they said to him, "If the prophet had bid thee do some great thing, wouldst thou not have done it? how much rather then, when he saith unto thee, Wash and be clean!"

The sound reason of this appeal brought Naaman to his senses. And he went to the River Jordan, and he bathed there seven times, and he was restored to health, just as Elisha had promised.

This time he came to Mount Carmel with gifts and offerings of boundless gratitude, with silver and gold and precious gems. But he quickly learned that the grace of God cannot be bought, for Elisha refused to take a single gift. Indeed, he considered it sacrilegious to accept rewards for God's mercy, and he told this to Naaman.

The captain was deeply impressed. And he exclaimed, "Thy servant will henceforth offer neither burnt-offering, nor sacrifice, unto other gods, but unto the Lord."

If Elisha would accept no reward, then perhaps he might accept a convert. This Elisha accepted, with an open heart.

And Naaman returned whole to Syria, a convert to the God of the Jews.

The devotion of a humble maid of Israel was instrumental, then, in the healing of an idolator, and in the making of a convert. Her heartfelt pity, even for the man who held her in subjection, set in motion a process that brought prophets and kings into conflict, into grace, and into miraculous resolution. Torn from her homeland, but remembering the teachings of her faith, and the powers of her God, she did not waver, in the idolator's house, from the straight line of her religion. The Hebrew tradition of pity and mercy was still within her, to be exercised towards countryman as well as towards the foreigner, and mercy flowed from her when confronted with her oppressor's plight.

We read no more of the maid of Israel, but it is evident that, though she may never have returned to her homeland, she had brought her homeland to Syria.

Jezebel

The deleterious influence of idolatry on the Hebrew social and political structure has already been noted. Monotheism, with strong underpinnings provided by the patriarchal family unit, could not have survived had not idolatry, with its fragmenting effects on the family, been eradicated among the Jews. One woman, more than any other character in the Old Testament, symbolizes the profound threat to Hebrew society which idolatry presented. She has been called the "heathen queen," and worse; and even more than Delilah's, her name has become synonymous with seductress, with sexual evil, and with licentiousness of the most horrendous sort. Indeed, there is no name more evil to the ear than that of Jezebel.

In Delilah's biography we saw that the Bible does not condemn so much as witness that infamous woman, and that, considering Samson's flawed character, there were, in her case, what might be called extenuating circumstances. But in Jezebel's portrait we confront the problem of evil in almost naked form, and find the authors of the Old Testament turning their harshest light upon this woman.

She was one of those who "bowed the knee to Baal"; in point of fact, her father was a high priest in the worship of Astarte, female counterpart of Baal in the religion of the Canaanites. Not born, then, as a Hebrew, she came, like Delilah, as a stranger among the Jews. But unlike Delilah, she came of her own will and, again unlike Samson's wife, did not center her cruel powers on only one man: the whole of Israel was Jezebel's target. And her ultimate goal was to dismantle Hebrew society by destroying belief in the "one sole invisible God." Her frenetic and violent attempts in this regard involved the monarchy itself and the prophets Elijah and Elisha, and struck at the very roots of Hebrew society and culture.

It is hard indeed to accept the fact that unalloyed evil burns in the hearts of some human beings. The severity with which Scripture treats of this woman leads us to infer, however, that such is, in fact, the case. But even here we encounter circumstances which, if not exactly extenuating do at least go some way towards explaining the phenomenon of a woman like Jezebel.

The ancient world teemed with conflicting religions and social orders. We have seen the many struggles in which the Jewish nation was involved because of inevitable differences with idolatrous societies. Deborah, we noted, raised her splendid standard not only for religious but for *political* reasons. That prophetess perceived the destructive social effects of idolatry upon Judaism, and roused her people to resistance. For it was not simply that the Jews *preferred* to believe in one God; that belief underlay their whole existence as a tribe. For without monotheism, and the secure family unit that went along with it, Jewish society would have dissolved and passed away, like idolatrous societies before it.

Thus, in Scripture we see Jezebel characterized as more than an individual: she is seen as a force wreaking havoc upon Jewish traditions and upon Jewish social survival. She is the symbol, then, of a power viewed as necessarily evil, for she aimed at the heart of Judaism, and she aimed to kill. Not incidentally, she manipulated contradictions which had grown to dangerous proportions within Jewish society itself under the monarchy.

Egalitarian democracy, which is so much a part of the Mosaic intention, had all but disappeared by the time King Ahab took the Canaanite woman Jezebel for his wife. True, the law was still in effect, and the people might seek justice from their king; but the justice they received, if they received it at all, depended entirely upon the character of the man who occupied the throne. Decisions and depositions might be wise or whimsical, subject to whether it was Solomon or Ahab who donned the robes of state. The responsibility of the whole people had been abdicated in favor of a monarchial figure who did not attain his station because of merit or intrinsic wisdom—like the patriarchs, for example, or the judges—but who rose to the fore by dint of inheritance or force.

The social equality envisioned by Moses, and which infused his law, had become subject to the accidents of history. Jezebel knew this, and she understood only too well the unreasonable power of the monarch among the Jews. As queen, she was in a position to deal with Jewish society in the most debilitating way, for the very fact of the monarchy had laid the groundwork beneath her feet.

There are, therefore, a number of penetrating questions which the Old Testament raises in the story of this woman, even in the midst of its harsh condemnation of her. And these questions reflect not only upon the conduct of this heathen queen, but upon the nature of the Jewish sociopolitical structure as well. For how was it that Ahab took to wife a woman who, unlike Ruth, would not renounce her own religion and take the one God to her heart? Was this marriage the result of an all too human lust on Ahab's part? And why was there no recourse to the law under Ahab when Jezebel's actions became unbridled? Obviously, Ahab acted as he chose, and beyond the law, for such was the king's power during this period. There was no human passion in his actions, for it was a cold political alliance he sought, in order to bolster Israel's dwindling military position. Evidently the law was an instrument to be used or not used as the monarch saw fit.

The Jewish state was at a very low point. There could have been no Queen Jezebel, after all, under Abraham or Moses.

Another matter raised by Jezebel's story is the role of sexuality in ancient Jewish society. Of course, when the Bible accuses Ahab's queen of licentiousness, a good deal more than sexual license is implied. But the fact remains that woman's power is often seen as a sexual force. Delilah, we saw, wielded her cruel power over Samson by playing upon his lusts. Rachel had a special place in Jacob's heart by dint of his warm and passionate affection for her. And woman's sexual power plays a large part in the stories of Hagar, Tamar, Dinah, and Ruth, though each was to use her attraction in a distinct way. Thus, looking at the Bible as a whole, it cannot be maintained that Judaism considered sexuality an evil force, for nothing could be more beautifully portrayed than Jacob's burning love for Rachel or Boaz's lawful and respectful passion for Ruth; and the fervor with which these women returned such passion was one of their finest qualities. And in Tamar's story we find a sexual narrative of both dignity and sly humor. Sexuality is seen in Scripture, then, as a force either for good or for evil, given the character of the persons involved. Of course, the violence of sex is there in Dinah's story, and its destructive influence clearly pictured for us in the figures of Delilah and Jezebel, but obviously the negativity of sex is by no means the only face the Old Testament puts upon human passion. It is beautiful or horrendous depending upon how it is used, and no evidence of an intrinsic fear of sex may be found in the Scriptures. Above all, woman herself is not seen as a fearful receptacle of man's weakness, as an evil snare; rather, woman's sexual nature is seen in the Bible as beautiful when not distorted by political schisms or by man's brute outrage.

In the case of Jezebel, the political implications of her licentiousness are evident. In order to break down the structure of the Jewish state, she employed sexual excess, among other crimes. Her intentions were not passionate but *cold*, and she was in deadly earnest, not in the throes of uncontrollable desire. Hers was a calculating nature, and nothing could be further from the sexual vulnerability of human nature than her manipulative behavior. She came to Ahab as a force already dedicated to destruction, and she set out to misuse her own womanly nature, and to violate the dignity of others.

It is important to consider these matters when one approaches the vile narrative of Jezebel's reign, for she was a woman of a certain time and place, a distorted age in many respects, and her actions reflect the general condition, albeit in highly colored, even lurid, tones.

We have already noted, in the maid of Israel's story, Ahab's incontinent character; we have also noted that the Syrian king looked upon the Hebrew prince as a vassal. It struck Ahab, then, as a politic move, to bring a Canaanite queen to his capital at Jezreel, thereby binding a more powerful military presence to Israel, whose position was faltering. And to Ahab and his advisers it may very well have seemed cunning. But so lacking was this royal class in any true knowledge of reality that they did not even consider the fact that the Canaanites looked upon Israel with more enmity than did the Syrians and, in the form of the lascivious Jezebel, were sending a viper into the Hebrews' midst.

Jezebel introduced her idols and her rituals into the Jewish court; she played upon the weakest instincts of her flawed lord, and encouraged waste and wantonness among the wealthier classes. So powerful was her impact upon Hebrew society that the prophet Elijah foretold dire events for the nation as a result of the conduct of Ahab's idolatrous queen. To Ahab Jezebel pronounced scorn for the troublemaking man of God, and chided him for his fears and manipulated his overweening self-esteem. Ahab was taken in, as always, by the superior wit of his wife, and ignored the portents of disaster with which Elijah was bombarding the land. It was to his everlasting folly that the king was convinced, at last, to persecute the prophets of God.

> There was a sore famine in Samaria. And Ahab called Obadiah, which was the governor of the house. (Now Obadiah feared the Lord greatly: for it was so, when Jezebel cut off the prophets of the Lord, that Obadiah took an hundred prophets, and hid them by fifty in a cave, and fed them with bread and water.) And Ahab said unto Obadiah, Go into the land, unto all fountains of water, and unto all brooks; peradventure we may find grass to save the horses and mules alive, that we lose not all the beasts.
> So they divided the land between them, to pass throughout it: Ahab went one way by himself, and Obadiah went another way by himself.

In his search, Ahab encountered the very prophet whom he had hounded more fiercely than all others— Elijah himself.

"And it came to pass, when Ahab saw Elijah, that Ahab said unto him, Art thou he that troubleth Israel?"

And Elijah replied, "I have not troubled Israel; but thou, and thy father's house, in that ye have forsaken the commandments of the Lord, and thou hast followed Baalim. Now therefore send, and gather to me all Israel unto Mount Carmel, and the prophets of Baal four hundred and fifty, and the prophets of the groves four hundred, which eat at Jezebel's table."

> So Ahab sent unto all the children of Israel, and gathered the prophets together unto Mount Carmel. And Elijah came unto all the people, and said, How long halt ye between two opinions? if the Lord be God, follow Him: but if Baal, then follow him. And the people answered him not a word. Then said Elijah unto the people, I, even I only, remain a prophet of the Lord; but Baal's prophets are four hundred and fifty men. Let them therefore give us two bullocks; and let them choose one

bullock for themselves, and cut it in pieces, and lay it on wood, and put no fire under: and I will dress the other bullock, and lay it on wood, and put no fire under. And call ye on the name of your gods, and I will call on the name of the Lord; and the God that answereth by fire, let him be God. And all the people answered and said, It is well spoken.

Jezebel was contemptuous of this contest. She had allowed the national gathering, no doubt, simply to placate the rising and dangerous gall of the Hebrew people, suffering as they were in the deepest throes of famine. And besides, she had no fear that her splendid priests would outshine the ascetic, wretched-looking man of God. Thus, she looked upon Elijah's challenge as contemptible and stupid, and upon Elijah as a madman.

What follows is a graphic description of an idolatrous rite.

And they took the bullock which was given them, and they dressed it, and called on the name of Baal from morning even until noon, saying, O Baal, hear us. But there was no voice, nor any that answered. And they leaped upon the altar which was made. And it came to pass at noon, that Elijah mocked them, and said, Cry aloud; for he is a god; either he is talking, or he is pursuing, or he is in a journey, or peradventure he sleepeth, and must be awakened. And they cried aloud, and cut themselves after their manner with knives and lancets, till the blood gushed out upon them.

And it came to pass, when midday was past, and they prophesied until the time of the offering of the evening sacrifice, that there was neither voice, nor any to answer, nor any that regarded.

Elijah then called the people to him: "Come near unto me." And they gathered around him, and watched as he built an altar out of twelve stones, representing the twelve tribes of Israel. It was an altar of the one God of their forebears, representing all that the people had forsaken under Jezebel's influence—the national unity, the sense of divine mission, the tradition of probity, equality, and familial order. Elijah drenched this altar with water, to forestall any charges of deception or trickery.

Then the hour of the evening sacrifice arrived. The lone prophet of God stepped before the altar he had built, in full view of his people, and called out, "Lord God of Abraham, and Isaac, and Jacob, let it be known this day that thou art a God in Israel, and that I am thy servant, and that I have done all these things at thy word. Hear me, O Lord, hear me, that this people may know that thou art the Lord God that hast turned their hearts back again."

Flames fell from heaven at his words, and consumed the burnt sacrifice, and the wood, stones, and dust. The people saw all this, and fell to their faces in the dust, and cried: "Jehovah—he is God! Jehovah is God!" And Elijah commanded, "Take the priests of Baal: let not one escape." And the people rose up, captured the idolatrous priests, and led them to the River Kishon, where they slew them, one and all.

And in the heavens the rainclouds gathered, at last portending a cessation of the famine. Elijah rejoiced, and told his king, "Prepare thy chariot and get thee down, that the rain stop thee not."

> And it came to pass that the heaven was black with clouds, and there was a great rain. And Ahab rode and went to Jezreel; and the hand of the Lord was upon Elijah, and he girded up his loins and ran before his [the king's] chariot to the entrance of Jezreel.

Jezebel, who had fled to Jezreel before her lord, was haughty and scornful when she heard of her priests' ignominious end, and of the miracles performed by Elijah. When she met with Ahab, who was flushed and awestruck at the things he had seen, she was contemptuous of him, and of his renewed faith. So pronounced was her character, so strong was her contempt, that the ever-vacillating Ahab was cowed.

The queen sent, then, a message to Elijah, flaunting her power even in the face of divine miracles. "So let the gods do to me," she told the prophet, "if I make not thy life as one of them by to-morrow." Ahab, she knew, would not protect the man of God, for the king was putty in her hands. So in spite of the revelation, she continued the persecution of the Lord's servants, and Elijah went wandering into the wilderness, in exile and fear of his life. Queen Jezebel was, then, the reason for his harsh sojourn in the desert, where he was to know hardship and privation of the worst sort; but he was to find, too, communion with his God.

During his absence, the outrages of Jezebel reached fever pitch. In spite of the suspicions and enmity of the masses of Jews, she set about the business of consolidating her political power. The wealthier classes were already under her sway, and the court continued to worship Baal, to perform superstitious and detestable rites, and to carry out her orders. She drew the law courts also into her sphere, and made of them puppets. There was no general on the order of Jephthah to obstruct her growing power, for the armies of her own land, Canaan, were sufficient to humble the military powers of Israel. She was free to move as if in a vacuum; Ahab was the figurehead and she, Jezebel, was the ruler.

The incident of Naboth's vineyards is perfectly illustrative of her vicious distortion of the law. Ahab, free to enjoy the indolent pleasures of his position, now that the affairs of state were firmly in the queen's hands, had little to do but covet the things that struck his fancy. And one of the things he most desired was the vineyard of Naboth, an itinerant and nearly bankrupt landowner. The vineyard was adjacent to Ahab's gardens, and he wished to expand the royal park. So he went to Naboth and offered the man money for the coveted land. "And Naboth said to Ahab, The Lord forbid it me, that I should give the inheritance of my fathers unto thee."

Obviously this Naboth, though poor, was "with God," for he shrank from alienating his own property—from, that is, violating the Mosaic code.

And Ahab came into his house heavy and displeased. And he laid him down upon his bed, and turned away his face, and would eat no bread. But Jezebel his wife came to him, and said unto him, Why is thy spirit so sad, that thou eatest no bread? And he said unto her, Because I spake unto Naboth the

Jezreelite, and said unto him, Give me thy vineyard for money; or else, if it please thee, I will give thee another vineyard for it; and he answered, I will not give thee my vineyard.

And Jezebel his wife said unto him, Dost thou now govern the kingdom of Israel? arise, and eat bread, and let thine heart be merry; I will give thee the vineyard of Naboth the Jezreelite.

One can imagine the woman's laughing at her husband's weakness when she spoke these words. She was used to humoring him, in order to keep him transfixed by his own petty desires, so that she might rule without his stupid interference. And it was a minor matter for her, this vineyard business, for she wielded the royal signet in her husband's stead, and controlled the judges, juries, and witnesses of the law courts. She had only to command her servants and they would obey.

So a travesty of justice was organized, and Naboth was brought to trial on trumped-up charges, bought witnesses blackening his good and simple character. Jezebel's carefully oiled political machine worked its inexorable evil, and the poor but proud Naboth was tried and condemned.

No more disreputable illustration of Jezebel's destructive impulses can be found. She was striking in this case at one of the most basic of Mosaic laws. To sell, to alienate property, was forbidden; one exchanged money for land only within families, and then the price was regulated by law, so that the transaction was more in the nature of giving. To speculate, to treat inheritance as barter, was to undermine Jewish social structure; thus, in executing Naboth, Jezebel gave warning that the alienation of property was, in fact, the law of the land, and all had best take heed, for a man was as good as dead should he refuse to set the law of Moses at naught. Jezebel had, then, special reasons of her own for pleasing her lord in this matter.

The queen told Ahab, "Arise, and go and take possession of the vineyard of Naboth, which he refused to give thee for money; for Naboth is dead."

And it came to pass, when Ahab heard that Naboth was dead,

that Ahab rose up to go down to the vineyard of Naboth the Jezreelite, to take possession of it.

This was, of course, only one more crime in Jezebel's impressive array of ugly outrages. Her religion had undermined the faith and egalitarian tendencies of the Jewish people; her sexual immorality had decimated the family structure, especially among the upper classes, among whom she was so fashionable; and she was turning the Mosaic law upon its head, so as to destroy the last tie of the Hebrews with their God, with the covenant of decency and fairness. But this matter of Naboth seemed to constitute the last straw, and to bite deeply into the Hebrew consciousness; for God called Elijah out of his meditation in the wilderness.

And the word of the Lord came to Elijah the Tishbite, saying, Arise, go down to meet Ahab king of Israel, which is in Samaria; behold, he is in the vineyard of Naboth, whither he is gone down to possess it. And thou shalt speak unto him, saying, Thus saith the Lord, Hast thou killed, and also taken possession? And thou shalt speak unto him, saying, Thus saith the Lord, In the place where dogs licked the blood of Naboth shall dogs lick thy blood, even thine.

And of Jezebel, God said, "The dogs shall eat Jezebel by the wall of Jezreel. Him that dieth of Ahab in the city the dogs shall eat; and him that dieth in the field shall the fowls of the air eat."

God had spoken, and Elijah obeyed. Boldly—for he knew the hand of the Lord was upon him—the prophet went out of the desert and entered the city of Jezreel, where a sentence of death hung over his head. But he looked neither to the right nor to the left, and no one impeded him. He was issued forthwith into the garden of his king, and there stood before Ahab.

And Ahab said to Elijah, Hast thou found me, O mine enemy? And he [Elijah] answered, I have found thee; because thou hast sold thyself to work evil in the sight of the Lord.

And he told the king of God's words, and the king drew back; but there was no hiding from the will of the Lord. The people themselves had been roused by the excess and impiety of the odious reign of this Ahab, and he was dragged soon thereafter to the place of Naboth's execution, and there the dogs did indeed lick his infamous blood.

But Jezebel ruled on, even after the death of the prophet Elijah. Still, God's word would not be obstructed; and in her wickedness, her arrogance, and her oppression of the people she insured her own doom. But among the terraces and turrets of the royal palace, insulated by her guards, by the wealthy, by the bought law courts, and by the threat of her own Canaanite army, she could look down, even now, upon the city, and spit out her contempt for the Jews. Her licentiousness continued unabated; the priests of Baal infested the palace; the upper classes were led deeper into debt and degeneration, just as before; and nothing had changed except that the degree of depravity was amplified.

Inevitably, rebellion clamored in the land. And two men rose up to give direction to the people's sense of anger and outrage. One of these was Jehu, the avenger, who drew about him an army of dissident Jews ready to fight and die in order to repair the cracks in the honor of the Jewish state. The other was the young prophet Elisha, a man, as we have seen, of great holiness.

There were these times in Hebrew history when the excess of the times paradoxically purified the Jewish spirit, shutting out all the idols and false ways they might have been following, and steeling them for vengeance against the symbols of their own sin. Elisha, like Elijah before him, was a powerful force in rousing the guilt and anger of the people, and of prodding them back to an understanding of their own traditions. In this time of the darkest evil, perpetrated by a people in the thrall of an evil queen, his voice struck terror in the hearts of all who heard him. And thus God's hand was laid upon Elisha, and he was called to anoint the avenger, Jehu, and to further the inexorable will of the Lord.

So the young man, even the young man the prophet, went to Ramothgilead. And when he came, behold, the captains of the host were sitting; and he said, I have an errand to thee, O captain. And Jehu said, Unto which of all of us? And he said, To thee, O captain. And he arose, and went into the house; and he poured the oil on his head, and said unto him, Thus said the Lord God of Israel, I have anointed thee king over the people of the Lord, even over Israel. And thou shalt smite the house of Ahab thy master, that I may avenge the blood of my servants the prophets, and the blood of all the servants of the Lord, at the hand of Jezebel. For the whole house of Ahab shall perish; and I will make the house of Ahab like the house of Jeroboam the son of Nebat, and like the house of Baasha the son of Ahijah; and the dogs shall eat Jezebel in the portion of Jezreel, and there shall be none to bury her. And he [Jehu] opened the door and fled.

This was the word for which Jehu and his men had been waiting. They marched for the capital, and all Jezebel's purchased guards fell before them, and all fear of the queen's Canaanite connections dissipated. The hand of the Lord was now upon Jehu, and nothing could deflect him from the single-minded furtherance of the Lord's word.

At last he and his band encountered the prince, Joram, born of Ahab by Jezebel.

And it came to pass when Joram saw him [Jehu], he said, Is it peace Jehu? And Jehu said, What peace, so long as the whoredoms and witchcrafts of thy mother Jezebel are so many? And Jehu drew a bow with his full strength, and smote Joram, and the arrow went out at his heart, and he sunk down in his chariot. Then said Jehu to his chief captain, Take him up and cast him on the portion of Naboth the Jezreelite.

The avenging army swept on, then, for the capital. Jezebel saw them coming from her lofty turrets, and had received word already of the death of her son. She was neither grief-stricken nor afraid, for such emotions did not reside in her cold breast. She had plotted the downfall of all Israel and now saw her own downfall approaching.

She knew that an attempt to escape would be fruitless. And besides, she still had faith in her own cunning, and would, she thought, seduce this Jehu and continue in her destruction of the Jewish nation. Her calculating mind and hard loveliness combined to convince her that God himself was but a slavering lecher, like the god she did herself worship, like the priests and rich Jews she did herself manipulate.

> And when Jehu was come to Jezreel, Jezebel heard of it, and she painted her face, and tired her head, and looked out at a window. And as Jehu entered in at the gate, she said, Had Zimri peace, who slew his master? And he [Jehu] lifted up his face to the window, and said, Who is on my side? who? And there looked out to him two or three eunuchs. And he said, Throw her down. So they threw her down; and some of her blood was sprinkled on the wall, and on the horses; and he trode her under foot. And when he was come in [the palace], he did eat and drink, and said, Go, see now this cursed woman, and bury her; for she is a king's daughter. And they went to bury her; but they found no more of her than the skull, and the feet, and the palms of her hands. Wherefore they came again, and told him. And he said, This is the word of the Lord, which He spake by his servant Elijah the Tishbite, saying, In the portion of Jezreel shall dogs eat the flesh of Jezebel; and the carcass of Jezebel shall be as dung upon the face of the field in the portion of Jezreel; so that they shall not say, This is Jezebel.

And thus the Old Testament, in one of its harshest judgments, rings down the curtain on this narrative.

Yet in the midst of the ugliness, excess, and bloodshed of this tale there burns the conviction that Israel had sunk to the depths of degradation and was to be roused from the torpor of her sin. That Jezebel had come among the appointed people of the Lord was proof that the nation had completely lost its faith and its will. Only in Elijah and Elisha, and in all the thundering prophets, could the Lord's wrath be brought home to the dissolute Hebrews. And what the people viewed in the death of the Canaanite queen, ruler of

Israel, was the culmination of their own violent transgressions; and when the dogs tore at the woman's dead body, the Hebrews saw their own sin being rent. It is a scene of such garish cruelty that the heart stops; then we remember that this was a desperate and vicious time, and that this woman had very nearly fulfilled her nightmare vision of a desiccated Israel.

Jezebel reigned at the nadir of the period of the monarchy, probably the least lawful epoch in Jewish history.

Jehosheba

When, in the tale of Jezebel, we read that Jehu struck down Joram the prince before marching on to fulfill the Lord's final, bloody injunction against the house of Ahab, we referred to a brief, violent skirmish that involved also the king of Judah, Ahaziah, who had joined forces, for political reasons, with Joram. This king, like Jezebel's son, was killed during the skirmish with the avenger's men, leaving Judah ruled by his wife, Athaliah, a queen quite as vicious as Jezebel, if not so thoroughgoing in her crimes. This monarchial period was rife with corrupt royalty; indeed, had it not been for the heroism of Ahaziah's sister, Jehosheba, the cruel Athaliah would have ruled unchecked.

Jehosheba was a woman of great and good qualities, and was tenderly attached to her brother. She had watched in horror as Ahaziah fell more and more beneath the power of his treacherous wife, and had deeply regretted his alliance with Jezebel's son, an alliance she knew to be the result of Athaliah's urgings. Still, she wept sorely for her brother. She was a godly woman; she was, in fact, wife to Jehoiada, priest of the temple, and lived with him within the precincts of the holy house.

When the shock of her brother's death finally left her, she began to worry over the fate of her nephews, the princes. For she knew that Athaliah was no sort of mother to these children of tender years, and she wished fervently to take charge of them, for to them she was very much attached. Issuing, then, from her period of mourning, she approached her husband and asked about the princes' condition.

Jehoiada told her the dire truth, from which he had shielded her during her bereavement. Athaliah had imprisoned the princes in the palace.

Jehosheba did not see the writing on the wall because of her innately good nature. She was not able to believe that even as wicked a woman as Athaliah would have still darker designs. Jehosheba fell to weeping, and asked whether it would be possible to go to the queen and seek to change the royal decree. Of course, Jehoiada knew such an act would be futile, and he told her so.

Then Jehoiada turned from his weeping wife and repaired to the temple, where he bent himself in prayer to his God, entreating Him to look with pity upon Judah and avert from it the gathering evil. For Jehoiada had not disclosed to Jehosheba the fact that Athaliah had imprisoned the princes in order to massacre them.

That night, Jehosheba, unable to sleep, arose and walked in the courtyard in front of the temple. Doubtless she was in the process of deep thought about the plight of her nephews, especially the youngest, Joash, then just a year old. Suddenly the sound of rattling armor broke the silence of the night. Ascending the wall, Jehosheba beheld a troop of soldiers entering at the palace gate. Soldiers in the middle of the night? All at once she realized what her husband, out of pity for her, had left unspoken. A sudden shriek startled the stunned woman, and she turned towards the palace, where she could dimly perceive a miserable scene: from the balconies and terraces of the women's apartment, children and females rushed about in the wildest fright. Soldiers pursued them, and Jehosheba recognized them now as the queen's own guard, who were notorious for performing every bloody deed the queen asked them to perform.

The princess knew only too well at that moment the designs of the ruler of Judah. But she could not stand by, looking on, without helping her nephews. The wailing increased from the women's quarters, and Jehosheba determined, at whatever risk to herself, to reach the palace.

There was a private way, built by Solomon, which led to the palace; and over this Jehosheba rushed, fearing nothing and no one. She sought the women's apartments, and found the place filled with soldiers, who barred her entrance.

"Away!" she told them boldly. "I am the princess Jehosheba."

The soldiers gave way before her command. And upon entering the chambers, a dreadful sight met her eyes. Dead and dying children, and nurses who had faithfully defended them, were lying, bloodied, at the feet of brutal soldiers. Jehosheba struggled through the horrendous scene in order to find the infant Joash. All had been killed except those in the last apartment.

Two faithful eunuchs stood before this last apartment, resisting the soldiers. They told Jehosheba to flee. She was undaunted, and pushed through the swords, becoming wounded in the process. Once inside the chamber, she looked wildly around, and espied a nurse clutching to her breast the infant Joash, the last remaining son of Ahaziah. Jehosheba seized the babe, and, concealing it under her wrapper, beckoned the nurse to follow. They rapidly made their way from the room. The faithful eunuchs were dead, and the soldiers, busy with their work, cared not to stop her, for they had been ordered to slaughter only the royal children. Struggling through the carnage, Jehosheba made her way back to the temple.

And at the temple Jehoiada was roused, and he rose to behold his beloved wife, bloodied and in a swoon, a trembling nurse, and the infant heir to the throne of Judah.

Now, Athaliah was as much an idolatress as Jezebel had been, and in these dark monarchial days few approached the temple of the Lord; thus, it was a place well suited for the hiding of the prince. Indeed, years passed, and the secret was known only to Jehosheba and her husband. They awaited a fortuitous moment to restore the boy Joash to the throne.

During these years they saw the temple of God stripped of its finery, its utensils melted down for the barbarous altars of Baal. The queen, because of her rapacity, her cruelty, and her unlicensed passions, was now despised even by those whom she had jaded. But Athaliah was not so cunning as Jezebel had been, and knew not how to consolidate her power even in the face of mass disapproval. She was more vulnerable than she suspected, and no act of God was needed to bring her down.

Jehoiada, reading the discontent of the people, took preliminary steps towards a rebellion. He called to council some of the Hebrews he knew he could trust, and also some disaffected officers of the queen's army. After swearing them to secrecy in the temple, he revealed to them the fact of the existence of the royal prince. They rejoiced, and vowed to serve the prince and set him on the throne. They were dispatched to the towns and cities of Judah to collect all those who "had not bowed the knee to Baal," and all the dispersed and disgruntled, for the purpose of forming a striking force.

Jehoiada, on the pretext of a feast day, called these faithful to the temple. And before them all he presented Jehosheba and the boy Joash, and proclaimed the child the descendant of David.

And he said to them, "I have called ye here this day to know if ye shall serve Baal or Jehovah!"

The people answered as one, that they would follow the Lord God of Israel. And so Jehoiada anointed the prince, and placed the holy diadem on his head.

Of course, Athaliah had been informed of these doings by her spies. But of the true strength of the dissidents she had no idea. She hastened along Solomon's passage to the temple, thinking by her very presence to put an end to the seditious proceedings. She had no inkling that her own guards would not protect her.

When she came upon the scene, she found the people crowding to kneel and do homage to the son of David. Passion, unreasonable and violent, took possession of her, and she cried, "Treason! Treason!"

"Take the accursed woman hence," said Jehoiada, "and slay her without the temple."

Athaliah was slain, and Joash reigned in her stead. In later years, the people turned more to their old traditions in Judah, and blessed the king. But they blessed the good princess Jehosheba, too, for her heroism.

Huldah

In the midst of the sinful period of the monarchy, there ascended to the throne a child, Josiah, who was to become a monarch very different from his predecessors. "He did that which was right in the sight of the Lord, and walked in all the way of David his father, and turned not aside to the right nor to the left."

In the eighteenth year of his reign he gave orders for the repairing and beautifying of the house of God. In the performance of these orders the high priest discovered the book of the law, in which the Mosaic ordinances were contained. No more glaring proof of the depths of ignorance to which the Jews had fallen is offered us in the Old Testament; that the high priests themselves were in total darkness regarding the form of the law is shocking, and that the book itself was accidentally unearthed, like a relic, is tantamount to apostasy on a national scale.

Josiah, when he realized the shell that the religion of his forefathers had become, rent his clothes and sent for all the priests. He told them, in his rage, to "inquire of the Lord for me, and for all of Judah, concerning the words of the book that is found, for great is the wrath of the Lord that is kindled against us, because our fathers have not hearkened unto the words of this book, to do according unto all that which is written concerning us." The priests shook with fright. How were they to interpret this "relic"?

They sought a prophetess: "And Hilkiah the priest, and Ahikam, and Achbor, and Shaphan, and Asaiah, went unto Huldah the prophetess, the wife of Shallum, the son of the keeper of the wardrobe (now she dwelt in Jerusalem in the college), and they communed with her." We see in this passage that women, even in so horrendous a period, were accorded the highest prestige. Unlike Deborah beneath her palm, or Elisha in his wanderings, this prophetess was ensconced in the college; and because the officers of the king sought her without hesitation, as the only one of whom they could inquire of the Lord, we have no choice but to infer that her wisdom and piety had long been known and acknowledged in that seat of learning, Jerusalem.

The powers of prophecy were never entrusted to the undeserving, male or female. Superior virtue only could attract the hand of the Lord; that, and superior intelligence. Huldah's dwelling in the college presupposes a mind anxious and inquiring in the study of the law and a heart yearning to explicate and follow the statutes.

Huldah, then, waited for the word of God; she prayed that she might be vouchsafed some sign to relieve the public and private inquity into which her nation had fallen. She waited patiently for that sign, that vision, which might brighten the darkness of the Hebrew condition.

Finally, to the priests Huldah said, "Thus saith the Lord God of Israel: Tell the man that sent you to me, thus saith the Lord, Behold I will bring evil on this place and on the inhabitants thereof; even all the words of the book which the king of Judah hath read; because they have forsaken Me, and burnt incense to other gods, that they might provoke Me to anger with all the works of their hands, therefore My wrath shall kindle against this place, and shall not be quenched."

These words issued from Huldah with all the fire of prophecy, and yet she also addressed the priests with a softer tone:

> But to the king of Judah who sent you to inquire of the Lord, thus shall ye say unto him, Thus saith the Lord God of Israel, As touching the news which thou hast heard; because thy heart was tender, and thou hast humbled thyself before the Lord, when thou heardest what I spake against this place, and against the inhabitants thereof, that they should become a desolation and a curse, and hast rent thy clothes and wept before Me, I

also have heard thee, saith the Lord; behold, therefore, I will gather thee to thy fathers, and thou shalt unto thy grave in peace, and thine eyes shall not see all the evil which I will bring upon this place.

Huldah's harsh message was delivered, and because of his piety the king was to be spared the horror of what the prophecy portended. Huldah had done her duty by her God, had foreseen the awful fate of her nation, and had spoken, not meekly, but decisively and to the point. Hers was a judgment, as well as a prophecy, upon the nation, for too long had the law that bound the tribes together and secured them from dissolution been ignored or violated.

Huldah's words issued in the painful time of the Babylonian Captivity. Her great learning and perceptive heart combined to pronounce a dire sentence, a much deserved sentence, upon the nation.

Now, Huldah was a prophetess much like Deborah, with this difference: Deborah exercised her powers when Israel was under the direct guidance of God; Huldah flourished in a time when a cloud existed between the Hebrew God and his people. Still, the position of women had not been degraded, for it was to a woman that the power of prophecy had been given.

Esther

After the licentious and ungodly period of the monarchy, the Jewish nation disintegrated, and the period of the Dispersion ensued, during which the appointed people of the Lord were scattered over the world and placed in captivity and other oppressive circumstances. At the center of the Hebrews' struggle to retain their ancient identity, there is one woman who symbolizes the grace and courage—and the love of Jewish tradition—which Hebrew women, even in so dire and disorganized a time, were capable of exhibiting. Indeed, her name is synonymous with the festival of Purim, and her bravery and intelligence consecrated thereby, among all the Jews, today as in the past, wherever they reside. Esther, meaning "star," was surely one of the most remarkable women in history.

In the land of ancient Persia, throughout which many Jews had been dispersed, there reigned Ahasuerus, a monarch who, like his predecessors Darius and Xerxes, built for himself palaces and cities of surpassing splendor—indeed, the marvelous ruins at Persepolis give only the merest indication of the magnificence of the Persian empire at its height. Ahasuerus especially liked to hold feasts and festivals in honor of the wealth and might of his kingdom, and his capital at Shushan was often the site of lavish proceedings.

At one point, having debased, in one of his more jaded moods, his own queen, this Ahasuerus threw the capital into a ferment of feasting, for the nobles, as well as for the poeple, by a proclamation made throughout the provinces that all the fairest maidens were to be gathered together at the palace, that the monarch might choose from among them a new queen. The most beautiful and gracious of these maidens was the Jewess Esther, whom the king found so beautiful that he looked at no other. Esther "was brought unto the king's house, to the custody of Hegai, the keeper of the women."

Esther had been brought up under the care of Mordecai, a Benjamite who claimed noble descent from the house of Judah. This Mordecai had kept alive in his household the ancient ways and had kept to the law; indeed, his adoption of the orphaned Esther had been in direct compliance with Moses' injunction that the fatherless should be cared for by their countrymen.

This royal marriage was not in the least a pleasant circumstance from Mordecai and Esther's point of view. It not only pulled the girl from her beloved adopted father, but placed her in a house dedicated to alien gods, a house in which she was to reign as queen, removed by the exaltation of the Persian masses from all contact with the religion of her youth. She and Mordecai offered up prayers of lamentation to the "one sole invisible God."

But to have resisted or refused compliance would have meant instant death at the despot's hands. Ahasuerus had seen, and what he had seen he desired; needless to say, what he desired he would have, or know the reason why. Fear of him, and concern for his adopted daughter, caused Mordecai to tell Esther not to reveal her religion, for the position of the Jews under the Persians was no less precarious than that under other foreign yokes. But his paternal affection for her did not cease: "And Mordecai walked every day before the court of the women's house, to know how Esther did, and what would become of her." His child was removed from under his watchful protection, but his love was with her nonetheless, and Esther must have felt comforted in the consciousness that he was near.

Having by her gracious manners won the love of the king and his court, the girl was raised to the throne amid much pomp and splendor. She became surrounded by the trappings of state and luxury. But so strong had been her upbringing and her education in Judaism that her affections, habits, and yearnings all revolved around the house of her childhood. She had been torn from early associations by an imperious mandate and debarred by circumstance from the exercise of her faith, which she could follow in her heart only; and the degradation of her predecessor did not make her very secure even amid the luxury, for at a moment's notice she might be murdered or banished by a kingly whim. It was not a very happy station for a young girl, no matter how one views it.

Her unambitious spirit and gentle nature are evident: she asked for nothing except that which the chamberlain of the court appointed for her. This modesty of behavior soon made the king love Esther "above all the women, and she found grace and favor in his sight." Indeed, upon her ascension, the king placed the crown upon her head himself, and "made a great feast unto all his princes, and his servants, even Esther's feast." Even so wanton a monarch as Ahasuerus, apparently, could not resist the attraction of the girl's virtues and quiet intelligence; and her comely appearance only heightened the effect.

It was probably during the rejoicing attending the choice of

Esther as queen that Mordecai obtained a situation in the king's household. Affection and anxiety for Esther had no doubt been the incentive for this change in his life. There is a dignity about Mordecai shown in the simple fact of his concealing his relationship with the petted queen, and in the simple way he acted for the well-being of his adopted daughter, even in the midst of the intrigues of the Persian court. The great esteem in which Esther held him is proof enough of his good and pious nature.

"Esther had not yet showed her kindred, nor her people, as Mordecai had charged her: for Esther did the commandment of Mordecai, like as when she was brought up with him." Even though she enjoyed court life, Esther followed Mordecai's injunction not to reveal her faith, for she respected his word above that of all others. The great isolation of life in the palace kept her from seeing him for years; yet she forgot neither his word not her religion.

Mordecai, in his post at the court, once heard of a conspiracy against the king, and he imparted this information to Esther through trusted messengers. By her this information was "certified to the king in Mordecai's name"—an honor which Mordecai had not sought, but one which Esther was pleased to give him. It is evidence of the whimsical nature of the Persian king that Mordecai's instrumentality in this matter was to be forgotten; but we see here the great affection Esther continued to bear her adopted father.

Years passed, and in the court the rise to power of an Amalekite—the Amalekites were ancient enemies of the Jews—claimed the attention of Persia. This Amalekite, called Haman, rose through the special favor of the king above all the other princes of the realm, and he became a sort of prime minister in the government of the country. Ahasuerus came to rely more and more upon his word; and Haman's ego expanded proportionately. The other ministers and the courtiers vied with one another to do Haman homage, and to incur his favor. The palace was almost literally at his feet, and everyone under the man's power—everyone, that is, except Mordecai.

The law of the Jews strictly forbade all unseemly veneration of mortal man, for glory was God's and Mordecai would not bend his knee for advancement. To be sure, he was aloof from the crude reverence with which the court prostrated itself before Haman; and such aloofness did not, of course, escape Haman's notice.

The servants of the king spoke to Mordecai: "Why transgressest thou the king's commandment?" That is, they wanted to know why Mordecai would not obey the prime minister. Finally Mordecai told them, and revealed what he had enjoined Esther to conceal. Seeing that Mordecai "hearkened not to them, they told Haman, to see whether Mordecai's matters would stand, for he had told them that he was a Jew." This was a bold and fearless admission, and in accordance with Mordecai's nature. He had made no show of his religion when no necessity called for it; but now that some tenet of that religion had been violated, he spoke up and stood his ground.

Haman, full of wrath that anyone dared hold him in contempt, and an avowed enemy of the Jewish race since birth, decided on a signal revenge. That some connection existed between Mordecai and the queen was, no doubt, suspected by the prime minister: to attack Mordecai alone would therefore avail him little, as the old man would be protected by the crown. But the destruction of the *whole* Jewish population in Persia, if he could but procure the king's consent, would involve Esther (of whose influence he was very probably jealous) as well as the despised Mordecai. And the mandate, once gone forth, would, according to Persian law, be unalterable.

That nothing might fail him, Haman cast lots, according to the superstition of the time, to discern what month would be most favorable to his prospects. It was during the first month of the Persian year that he did this, and, as chance would have it, the lot fell on the last month. Haman looked upon the twelve-month interval as a good omen, for it would allow him time to plan the eradication of the Jews in even the remotest provinces of the empire. This interval was not to work in his favor, but it is a testament to his vile and bloody nature that his mind was filled with visions of universal destruction. His character, to be sure, reminds us of Nimrod and the pharoah.

He proceeded with consummate caution. Working upon jealousy, he alluded to a certain people, who, dispersed among all the king's provinces, followed a religion and laws of their own. He said that it was not to the king's profit that they do so. He insinuated, no doubt, that they were likely to turn others from their allegiance to the king and their gods. It would be wise, therefore, to have them destroyed. So that the king's coffers would not suffer, the wily minister concluded his counsel with a promise of ten thousand talents of silver for the royal treasury.

Ahasuerus was in instant accord with his minister's advice, and gave into Haman's hand the royal signet, to do with the people as he saw fit. Thus, the awful decree went out over all the vast domains of the empire, and consternation and mourning took possession of the hapless Jews, who—men, women, and children, the old and young—were condemned to be destroyed on the thirteenth day of the twelfth month. All their belongings were to become the spoil of their destroyers. Hemmed in by the king's armies, and having no Moses to lead them out of captivity, the Jews knew an overwhelming and desperate despair. Little did any of them suspect that it would be by a woman's influence that they would be saved, by a woman's intelligence and devotion. Nimrod and the old pharoah, at least, had condemned only the male issue of the Jews: this Haman would eradicate all of the Lord's appointed people at once. No one suspected that Hebrew tradition, and Hebrew continuance, had a formidable ally in the meek and circumspect queen.

> When Mordecai perceived all that was done, he rent his clothes, and put on a sackcloth with ashes, and went out into the midst of the city, and cried with a loud and bitter cry; and came even before the king's gate: for none might enter clothed in sackcloth. And in every province, whithersoever the king's commandment and his decree came, there was a great mourning among the Jews, fasting, and weeping, and wailing; and many lay in sackcloth and ashes.

All, then, who might have abused Mordecai for his long silence on the question of his religion, could not now accuse him. For he came in the sight of all as a Jew, and lamented the fate of his people. He approached the palace itself with his complaint, to show all, commoner and noble alike, that he sorely opposed the demise of tolerance in Persia.

Esther, meanwhile, continued in the seclusion of the palace—seeing no suffering, no poverty, and no disruption—and she continued, too, as the most beloved of Ahasuerus. But we have seen that royal retirement and luxury had not tarnished her love for her adopted father, nor for her childhood religion. Her feelings for Mordecai must have been suspected by her servants, for they immediately came to the queen's apartments with the strange news that Mordecai was clothed in sackcloth and ashes at the royal gates, apparently in the deepest affliction. That the king's decree had not been made known in the secluded chambers of the queen is evident—indeed, by custom in Persia, the king's wife was to know nothing of political and social matters, lest such information disturb her repose or mar her ornamental function. Thus, Esther had been kept ignorant of the nature of Mordecai's affliction. Nevertheless, she acted swiftly.

"Esther was exceedingly grieved; and she sent raiment to clothe Mordecai, and to take away his sackcloth from him: but he received it not." Neither did he convey to the queen the source of his unhappiness, and Esther, unable to follow the dicates of her own heart, sent another messenger to him, with her royal command, to know what it was, and why it was; thus blending the dignity of the queen with the affection of the child, and compelling his reply.

His silence at first may have issued from his long-standing desire to shield his adopted daughter from danger, for well he knew the precarious position of a Persian queen who dared meddle in social or political affairs. Her race and faith were still unknown—why, then, should he betray them at a time when their betrayal threatened death? The affection of a father struggled with the emotions of the patriot, but before the messenger left, Mordecai had made his decision. Imparting the designs of Haman, the decree proceeding therefrom, he sent a copy of the writing to Esther, charging her to go in unto the king, and supplicate him for her people. The very wording of this message revealed all, at last, and brought home to Esther that the decree extended to her as well as to *her people*. How forcefully, then, was the vaunted seclusion of the Persian queen shattered.

Esther's first reaction was fear, for she had been schooled, as queen, in the awful prerogatives of the king. She knew how swiftly would her royal life end should the king hold her in disfavor. Her predecessor had been banished on a whim; as a Jew, Esther would know a severer fate. Perhaps, indeed, she preferred to die along with her people rather than incur the king's wrath and wanton rage.

Esther sent her messenger back to Mordecai with these words:

> All the king's servants, and the people of the king's provinces, do know, that whatsoever, whether man or woman, shall come unto the king into the inner court, who is not called, there is one law of his to put him to death, except such to whom the king shall hold out his golden sceptre, that he may live: but I have not been called into the king's presence these thirty days.

Doubtless, then, the inroads of Haman into the royal favor had affected Esther's position as well; to stay away for so long was unlike Ahasuerus, who doted on Esther.

But Mordecai's plan had already been fixed, and his answer was instantly returned to the queen.

> Think not to thyself that thou shalt escape in the king's house, more than all the Jews. For if thou altogether hold thy peace at this time, then shall enlargment and deliverance arise to the Jews from another place; but thou and thy father's house shall be destroyed: for who knoweth whether thou art come to the kingdom for such a time as this?

From his words it is evident that Mordecai perceived Esther's ascension to the Persian throne to be in the nature of providence, a sign from his people's God that she had been torn from his bosom for just such a crisis as had befallen the Hebrews in their Persian captivity.

It is apparent that his confidence did not extend to his adopted daughter, though, with meekness, she gave no further resistance.

There is a deep and mournful essence that breathes in her answer, a hopelessness, and yet a devotion.

"Go," she replied by messenger, "gather together all the Jews that are present in Shushan, and fast ye for me, and neither eat nor drink three days, night or day: I also and my maidens will fast likewise; and so will I go in unto the king, which is not according to the law: and if I perish, I perish." And she turned and bade her maidens fast; and she settled down to pray. Her prayer is one of the most beautiful in all the literature of the world, containing the devotion and suffering which must have attended the woman during these dark days. This prayer is written in the Apocrypha, and because of its supreme loveliness, we quote it here in full:

And she prayed unto the Lord God of Israel, saying, O my Lord, thou only art our King. Help me, desolate woman, which have no helper but Thee. For my danger is in mine hand. From my youth up, I have heard in the tribe of my family, that Thou, O Lord, tookest Israel from among all people, and our fathers from all their predecessors, for a perpetual inheritance; and Thou hast performed whatsoever Thou dost promise them. And now we have sinned against thee; therefore hast thou given us into the hands of our enemies, because we worshipped their gods.

O Lord, Thou art righteous. Nevertheless it satisfieth them not that we are in bitter captivity; but they have stricken hands with their idols, that they will abolish the thing that Thou with Thy mouth hast ordained, and destroy Thine inheritance, and stop the mouth of them that praise Thee, and quench the glory of Thine house, and of Thine altar; and open the mouths of the heathen to set forth the praises of the idols, and to magnify a fleshly king for ever. O Lord, give not Thy sceptre unto them that be nothing; and let them not laugh at our fate, but turn their device upon themselves, and make him an example that hath begun this against us. Remember, O Lord, make Thyself known in time of our affliction, and give me boldness, O King of the nations, and Lord of all power. Give me eloquent speech in my mouth before the lion: turn his heart to hate him that fighteth against us, that there may be an end of him, and all that are like-minded with him. But deliver us with thine hand, and help me that am desolate, which have no other help but Thee.

Thou knowest all things, O Lord; Thou knowest that I hate the glory of the unrighteous and abhor the bed of the uncircumcised and the heathen. Thou knowest my necessity; for I abhor the sign of my high estate which is upon my head, in the days wherein I show myself, that I abhor it, and that I wear it not when I am private by myself. And that thine handmaid hath not eaten at Haman's table; and that I have not greatly esteemed the king's feast, nor drunk the wine of drink-offerings. Neither had thine handmaid any joy since the day I was brought hither to the present, but in Thee, O Lord God of Abraham. O Thou Mighty God, above all, hear the voice of the forlorn, and deliver us out of the hands of the mischievous, and deliver me out of my fear.

We see, then, that beneath the quiet graciousness that so endeared Esther to the court, there was a burning abhorrence of her station. She did not despise Ahasuerus as a man, but because he was an idolator who would not follow God's laws. It was to Haman that she wished the severest punishment God could mete out, because he not only ignored the law, but violated it, and thoroughly. All the luxury of the Persian court was nothing to Esther, and all its intrigues detestable.

Therefore, for three days, praying and fasting, she pondered and considered her course of action. And when at the end of this period of time she had chosen her plan, she carried it out with all the grace, circumspection, and quiet courage that have come down to us as hallmarks of her remarkable character, and that constitute her shining legacy.

She called her maidens and had herself clothed in gorgeous raiment, which enhanced her already extraordinary beauty. And then she courageously entered the king's chambers, disobeying the law of the Persian kings; but she did so with a delicacy, a refinement, that played upon the king's heart, and dissipated Haman's influence, and made Ahasuerus regret that he had so long neglected his lovely wife. Thus, instead of displaying anger at this unlawful encroachment, he held forth his sceptre towards her in instant exoneration, and she drew near and touched it, a sign that she implored a boon.

"What wilt thou, Queen Esther," he asked, "and what is thy request? It shall be even given thee, to the half of the kingdom."

Esther hesitated to voice her request, and merely said, "If it seem good unto the king, let the king and Haman come this day unto the banquet that I have prepared for him."

She had no intention of scuttling her plea by a too early boldness. And she was wise, indeed, to include Haman in her invitation, thereby putting whatever suspicions the prime minister may have entertained completely to rest.

The invitation was accordingly transmitted to Haman, and he and the king went in and partook of the banquet which Esther had prepared.

Again the king reiterated the inquiry and the promise: "What is thy petition? and it shall be granted thee: and what is thy request? even to the half of my kingdom it shall be performed."

And again, Esther simply replied, "If I have found favor in the sight of the king, and if it please the king to grant my petition, and perform my request, let the king and Haman come to the banquet that I shall prepare for them, and I will do tomorrow as the king hath said."

The graciousness for which Esther had become famous in the court shines from these words; and the king, smiling indulgently upon her, no doubt conceived that her request was a simple one, and that her much admired modesty—so much a part of her attraction for him—was at the heart of her reticence.

As for Haman, he left the queen's presence rejoicing and triumphant. He may very well have suspected her of having had some connection with Mordecai, but he did not, of course, dream that she, the monarch's wife, followed the dictates of Mordecai's God. Doubtless he felt that he had taken the queen's fancy, and that the plight of Mordecai was now a matter of indifference to her. He boasted to the other ministers of the queen's favor and conceived that he was, in fact if not in name, the most powerful person at the court. Did not the king follow his every suggestion? Had not Mordecai been effectually removed as a stumbling block from his path? And had not Mordecai's protector, the queen, now fallen under his sway, by extending not one, but two, invitations? His triumph, he thought, was complete. The fate of the enemy of his race, and the operations of the court itself, he carried about in his hands. Or so he supposed.

Yet, in the very midst of his triumph, as the prime minister left the palace, Mordecai, who still sat at the king's gate in his sackcloth and ashes, would not stand up as he passed, nor so much as move a muscle. Haman was enraged at this impertinence, proving that his riches, gratified ambition, regal favors, all availed him nothing, so long as the Jew sat so brazenly at the king's gate.

Haman arrived home in a gloomy state; his wife and servants, drawing from him the reason for his ill temper, suggested that the all-powerful prime minister have some gallows constructed near the palace, gallows at least fifty cubits high, upon which to hang the recalcitrant Jew for all to see. After all, Haman was clever, and he held, by his own admission, the operations of the court in his hands; it would be a small matter to concoct some tale, which he might take to the king the next day, so as to obtain his royal consent for the instant execution of the man he so thoroughly detested. That very night Haman dispatched workers to the palace to construct the gallows.

That night others were wakeful as well. The queen prayed, as earnestly as ever she had, for the grace of God in the matter of her plans. Thousands were destined to be slaughtered. If her plans did not work, who and what would arise to save them?

The king, too, could not sleep. And, to make himself drowsy, he commanded that the chronicles of the kingdom be read to him—a nice piece of irony in the biblical narrative, that this most whimsical of monarchs found not interest but only somnolence in the records of his own government. But the king found not sleep but unrest in the chronicles.

As the documents were unrolled, it so happened that the old

conspiracy against him, which Mordecai had uncovered, was droned into the royal ear. His long neglect of Mordecai now became a matter of some puzzlement to Ahasuerus: "What honor," he asked his servants, "hath been done to Mordecai for this?" Believing that Mordecai had been rewarded, the king could not understand the embarrassment into which he threw his servants.

"Then said the king's servants that ministered unto him, There is nothing done for him." The servants knew full well the enmity of Haman for Mordecai. For had they not been groveling before the prime minister, and heaping scorn upon the Jew, in order to curry favor? Suddenly, now that their wanton monarch had blundered onto the facts, they quailed before him. For who would be so incontinent as to inform the royal presence that he had himself signed a decree condemning not only Mordecai, but his whole people as well? The loss of one's life was a swift and simple matter under this Persian's regency. Were they to say to Ahasuerus, "Why, thou hast repaid Mordecai with death, and with the death of all his kind"? The king's rage at his own stupidity would sweep away at least seventy mere servants before he settled for bland contrition.

The distress of the servants was relieved by the fortuitous arrival of Haman, eager to settle the matter of Mordecai's execution in the dawning light of the morn. The puzzled king had his prime minister admitted forthwith.

"What shall be done," the king asked Haman at once, "unto the man whom the king delighteth to honor?" Because he had a one-track mind, this king could not believe that others did not share his every concern, and know his every thought in advance.

Naturally, puffed up with vanity, Haman supposed the king to be referring to him, the prime minister. Who can the king delight to honor more than me? he thought.

And so he advised a triumph which would make him second only to the king in the eyes of the masses. He was, of course, convinced that he was advising his own glorification, and in his crafty way, he threw in, as a vicious fillip, the words, "Do even so to Mordecai the Jew, who sitteth at the king's gate: let nothing fail of all that thou has spoken." In other words, to add to the prime minister's pleasure, the king might be so good as to carry out his decree against the Jews by prematurely executing Mordecai. The king agreed *wholeheartedly*, and shortly—to the Jew's amazement and the Amalekite's overwhelming chagrin—the figure of Mordecai was to be seen riding throught the streets of Shushan on a caparisoned charger, his wretched sackcloth covered with the plush robes of royalty, trumpets and hosannas echoing in his bewildered ears.

Thus, the royal capriciousness that had so long played into Haman's hands backfired in a splendid show of obtuseness, confusion, and misunderstanding. The king had not, of course, remembered his decree against the Jews, for he had given his signet without knowing the race he was condemning; that Mordecai was a Jew meant nothing to him, therefore, and he simple appropriated Haman's cruel advice into his own muddled whims.

Haman's rage cannot be imagined, as he heard the royal orders go out for the glorification of his enemy, when he had intended a death sentence to go out. But he was given little time to reflect on his own blunder, and upon the king's inordinate dizziness, for there arrived at that point the second of Esther's dinners. Thus he had to rush off to the queen's quarters, with no time for scheming.

Again the queen had assembled around her gorgeousness and festivity to gratify the luxurious tastes of the Persian king. Her beauty, heightened by successful adornment, concealing under graceful courtesy the indignation and fear which had riddled her nights, dazzled not only the king but the enraged Haman as well. And again the king reiterated his request and his promise.

This time Esther felt the ground had been properly prepared, and she played her last, and only, card. Boldly she replied, "If I have found favor in thy sight, O king, and if it please the king, let my life be given me at my petition, and my people at my request. For we are sold, I and my people, to be slain and to perish. If we had only been sold to slavery, I had held my tongue."

We know from her prayer that Esther hated idolatry and intrigue; but the passionate distaste she felt was tempered by a smooth and balanced wit. She had increased the king's expectations and curiosity with each invitation; she had set him up, as the saying goes, for a benevolent response; and she softened her request by saying that only the severity of the decree had prompted her petition. We may well wonder at her self-control before the king, and in spite of his caprices; for we know from her prayer that she could no more have seen her people in bondage than in the grave.

"Who is he," the king broke in, "and where is he that durst presume in his heart to do so?"

And Esther answered. "The adversary and enemy is this wicked Haman!"

Haman was stunned; he could see his own blunders and the queen's web closing in about him. The anger that might have fallen on the servants of the king that morning, when the monarch nearly discovered his own stupidity, was now hovering over the prime minister.

Ahasuerus rose up in a rage. Doubtless he considered himself the victim of ministerial duplicity, rather than the willing instrument of the destruction of a whole people, which is what he had been, after all, though he had not deigned to elicit the identity of the race he had favored with his wrath. In any case, by Persian custom, the king was never wrong, only misled; and the ministers had to bear the brunt of punishment when things went awry. Ahasuerus dashed from the queen's quarters and into the garden, ostensibly to quell the rage he felt towards Haman; more probably he was eager to hide his own embarrassment at having been such a frivolous fool. But then, how was he to know that he had condemned his favorite wife along with thousands of others? In his fuming in the garden he convinced himself, in any event, that those damnable ministers were at the bottom of it all.

Haman was, to be sure, a mass of quivering jelly after the king stormed from the banquet. He turned white, stood up, stumbled about, and fell in a swoon at the feet of Esther, who was reclining on a couch, in the customary repose of the Persian queen. And there Haman lay—not, we suspect, a very pleasant spectacle to Esther—until the king returned.

"What!" bellowed the monarch, upon viewing this scene, "will he force our queen also in our very presence?" (This Ahasuerus was, apparently, one of the denser of the Persian regents.)

At that moment an alert—and probably jealous—attendant, one who had long been awaiting the downfall of the insufferable Haman, piped up: "Behold the gallows, fifty cubits high, that he made to hang Mordecai, the saviour of the king's life."

And the king said, "Hang him thereon."

The royal command was instantly obeyed, and then only "was the king's wrath pacified."

Eager to make amends, the king gave to Esther the whole house and all the possessions of Haman. Then it was that Esther revealed her close relationship to Mordecai, and her faith; and Mordecai, fresh from his triumphal, if disorienting, procession through the town, came before the king, and received from his hand the signet which Ahasuerus had pulled from Haman's rotting finger, as a symbol that he was now prime minister in his enemy's place. "And Esther set Mordecai over the house of Haman."

It is gratifying to note, in the midst of these celebrations at the palace, that the plight of the Jews generally was, at one point, attended to. Having fallen prostrate at the feet of her lord, Esther besought him to put away the mischief of Haman—a difficult task, since in Persian law, once a royal decree was issued it could not be retracted.

"If it please the king, and if I have found favor in his sight, and the thing seem right before the king, and I be pleasing in his eyes"—Queen Esther had a flair for covering all eventualities, apparently—"then let it be written to reverse the letters devised by Haman, which he wrote to destroy the Jews which are in all the king's provinces; for how can I endure to see the evil that shall come unto my people? and how can I endure to see the destruction of my kindred?"

She could not have framed her petition in words more likely to reach the heart of the sovereign than those making the cause of the Jews so utterly her own cause. A simple entreaty for them as a people unjustly sentenced to universal destruction would not have been successful with *this* king; but because she identified herself with them, she was able to play upon his inordinate fondness for her.

Full permission was given to her and Mordecai to write as it pleased them, "for the writing which is written in the king's name, and sealed with the king's seal, might no man reverse." Scribes were accordingly summoned in all haste—scribes who could write in every language of the one hundred and twenty-seven provinces of the Persian empire, to the generals, deputies, and rulers.

Wherein the king granted the Jews which were in every city to gather themselves together, and to stand for their life, to destroy, to slay, and to cause to perish, all the power of the people and province that would assault them, little ones and women, and to take the spoil for their prey.

Copies of this strongly worded message were forwarded hastily by mule and by camel, pressed on by the king's commandment and imperious desire.

The apparent vindictiveness in this message devised by Esther and Mordecai was more or less necessary, for the king could not, by law, annul his previous decree, but could only issue another, which would make the enactment of the first one a matter of some trepidation to all those who might attempt to carry it out. The message was particularly intended to impress the Amalekites, who, sad to say, were rather more in favor of the first decree.

The bloodshed which ensued between the Jews and the Amalekites was not simply the result of their ancient enmity; rather, it was the idiotic machinery of the Persian state which tore open the old wounds. That a king's word could not be reversed was the sort of stricture which emanated from a belief in the sovereign as a god who could not make mistakes. Now, it is evident that Ahasuerus was about as infallible as a five-year-old; thus the Persian law worked, in this case, to the detriment of Persian society and against the peace of the realm. The violence of the struggle between the Jews and their age-old enemies had been directly provoked by the political vicissitudes of this bungling king.

The depth of animosity that existed between Jew and Amalekite is vividly pictured for us in the vengeance Esther herself took on the ten sons of Haman. Doubtless these sons had already been killed in the bloody disruptions which visited Shushan, and many other cities of the empire, upon the issuing of the second decree. But as a terrible example she had their bodies hung up upon the gallows for all to see. This is, to be certain, the first indication we have of the surfacing of Esther's resentment since her ascendance to the throne. Her prayer, with its undercurrents of contempt for the idolatrous and oppressive character of the state over which she ruled as queen, gives us a fairly accurate map of her true *inner* feelings, which were complex, indeed; but with the complete subjugation of the king to her demands, that inner contempt burst into the light of day, and gives some idea of the enormous self-control she must have exercised during the long years of her early reign. Injustice was for her a deep and wounding affront; her ornamental function as queen, a constant source of frustration; and her fears, and the intrigues which these fears inspired, during Haman's ascendency, a humiliation. She could turn as fierce and unforgiving as the patriarchs of old now that the restrictions on her person and position had been removed.

As to the disruptions, the Jews emerged victorious, and the Amalekites were humbled, and when not humbled, slaughtered. But that this slaughter had been provoked by the Amalekites themselves is evident from the wording of the second decree; for the Jews were enjoined to "stand for their life" only when threatened with hurt. To have initiated the hostilities would have violated the law, and neither the Perisna army nor the Persian courts would have upheld the Jews.

And we are told, too, not once but many times, that, though they had the right by law, "on the spoil laid they not their hand." It was enough that they were allowed to defend themselves, a privilege which, in the previous decree, they had been denied. To seek profit by a civil war was unthinkable to the majority of Jews in Persia, and the avidity with which Esther and Mordecai penned the second decree was rejected in the behavior of their countrymen. Fierceness and resentment were a part of Esther's character, and no doubt; but it is a shining reflection on the dispersed Jewish nation that they did not perpetuate these tendencies.

Esther's nature, like that of all the great women of the Old Testament, was, then, a complex one. Years of seclusion, of forced idleness and incapacity, had bitten deeply into her soul. Ripped, by the wanton desires of an idolatrous monarch, from the bosom and security of her family and placed like a plaster fixture at the head of state, she had found there, we know from her prayer, deep bitterness. But her cunning mind and quick wit had not ossified while she lounged in the queenly repose of the Persian court. When the time came for her to act, she acted swiftly and with intelligence. That a burning hatred pulsed beneath her royal graciousness and circumspection only enhances the woman's stature; for she was, we see, one of the righteous, one of those who knew and respected the law of Moses, at the side of which the Persians' legal caprice must have seemed crude, cruel, and barbarous. If she acted to excess it was because she had struggled against the excesses of the Persian state.

We are told that "Mordecai the Jew was next unto King Ahasuerus, and great amongst the Jews, and accepted by the multitude of his brethren, seeking the wealth of his people, and speaking peace to all his seed."

Esther's story concludes with the establishment of the festival of Purim, which is observed by all Jews throughout the world to the present day. The fourteenth and fifteenth days of Adar were ordained to be "remembered and kept throughout every generation, every family, every province, and every city; that these days of Purim should not fail from among the Jews, nor the memorial of them perish from their seed."

Judith

In the Apocrypha there is recounted a story that more than sums up, for our purposes, the dignity and heroism of womanhood that resulted from Mosaic institutions and laws. In the tale of Judith, the deliverer of her people during the odious Babylonian captivity, we find the huge reverence in which women were held by the Hebrew nation and by Hebrew tradition.

The Jews had a momentary respite from their various periods of captivity with the reconstruction of the altar at Jerusalem, and the old patriotism grew among the people again. But this tenuous rebirth was immediately threatened by the ascension of Nebuchadnezzar to the Assyrian throne. His empire was vast and he would brook no interference in imposing his iron will upon all the peoples of the realm. Indeed, he sent his bloodiest and most able general, Holofornes, to extend the Assyrian rule as far as possible; thus, the armies of Nebuchadnezzar laid waste to Mesopotamia, and scourged the plains of Damascus. Wheat harvests were trampled down, flocks and herds destroyed, cities spoiled, people slain. Many of the nations were overawed, and sued for peace. Ambassadors were sent to placate Holofornes, and to offer allegiance.

"Behold, we the servants of Nebuchadnezzar, the great king, lie before thee," said the ambassadors. "Use us as shall be good in thy sight. Behold our houses, our fields of wheat, our flocks and our tents lie before thy face, use them as it pleaseth thee. Behold, even our cities, and the inhabitants thereof are thy servants; come and do with them as seemeth good unto thee."

Thus, wherever he went, the Assyrian general saw all yield to his power, and he was welcomed with dances and timbrels, and crowned with garlands. These submissive cities were pardoned, but each received a garrison to enforce future allegiance to the Assyrian regent. And the gods of each land were destroyed, that all might worship the gods of Assyria.

The approach of this great army brought dismay to the hearts of Israel and Judah. Still, the idea of submission was repugnant to them, and they resolved never to bow down to the idolator's gods. Thus the Jews "cried to God with great fervency. The inhabitants of Jerusalem were clothed with sackcloth, and with ashes on their heads, remained night and day before the temple, fasting, and offering gifts to the Lord that He might show Himself." Joachim, the high priest at Jerusalem, and all his priests, "covered themselves and the altar with sackcloth, and cast ashes upon their mitres, and cried to God with all their power, that He would look upon the house of Israel graciously."

Holofornes's army was expected to pass through the hills of Galilee on their march to Jerusalem; thus, the strongholds of that area became vital for the defenses of Israel. The passes were fortified and supplied with food for a year's duration, while Bethulia, the most crucial of the Galilean cities, prepared itself for siege. The population of that city made a solemn oath even to sacrifice themselves before they would allow this lawless idolator to place his foot in their holy temple, so lately purified upon their return from captivity.

Holofornes found his first resistance in these mountain passes. His glorious career had now been, he felt, besmirched, and his rage grew accordingly. Having encamped, he tarried an entire month to gather around him all his chariots and horsemen to crush at once those rebellious hill forts which dared to resist him.

Bethulia, almost impregnable, was situated upon a hill near the Sea of Galilee, and it was the point towards which the Assyrian general decided to concentrate all his forces. A place of such defensive importance, should it fall, would serve as a warning and an intimidation to all the Jewish people, he reasoned, and would clear his path to Jerusalem.

Unused to resistance, Holofornes chafed at the delay. Fearing he would lose valuable time, he called a council of his officers and of the princes of the subjugated Canaan, to devise measures for the defeat of Israel.

"Tell me, ye sons of Canaan," he said, "who is this people that dwelleth in the hill country, and what are the cities they inhabit... what is the multitude of their army; what their power, and what king is set over them? Why come they not out to meet me, as do the cities around them?" It was indeed a puzzle to the general, how this small and obscure people could so courageously resist his might and the might of his arms.

One of the Canaanite princes answered, "The inhabitants of this land are great and powerful; they rely for protection on no king, but are governed and shielded by a great and wonderful God, who ever saveth them from harm, and revengeth them on those who go up to slay them."

Upon hearing the Jews' history from this prince, Holofornes was sorely puzzled. But this same prince then told him, "Let not my lord hope to subdue them while they obey their God. Now, therefore, my lord, if this people sin against their God, they will not prosper, and we may go up and overcome them."

Holofornes and his men were enraged that anyone should so much as suggest that the Assyrian army was not the most powerful on earth, or that there was any god but Nebuchadnezzar. The wily advice of this prince was ignored, and his person expelled from the camp: he was taken bound to the territory of Israel and there deposited.

The Israelites took the Canaanite prince into their midst and drew from him the story of what had transpired in the camp of Holofornes. Holofornes had expected the Jews to destroy this idolatrous prince, but wiser heads prevailed at Bethulia, and the information was duly considered, mulled over, and variously interpreted. Some fell to their knees at the idolator's description of the might and vast array of the Assyrians; other were more sanguine. In any event, prayers went up to heaven on behalf of the Hebrew nation, and there was a definite tendency to temporize.

"Lord God of Israel!" prayed the people, "pity the nation, and look down this day upon the face of those Thou hast sanctified."

At this point in the narrative we are told of a widow of some prominence at Bethulia, a widow whose influence was to be significant in the history of her people:

Now Judith was a widow in her house three years and four months. And she made her tent on the top of the house, put on sackcloth and wore her widow's apparel; and she fasted all the days of her widowhood, save the eves of the Sabbaths, the Sabbaths, and the new moons and solemn feast days of Israel. She was also of goodly countenance, and beautiful to behold, and her husband, Manasses, had left her gold and silver, and manservants and maid-servants, and cattle, and lands; and she remained upon them. And there was none gave her an ill word, for she feared God greatly.

Now, Ozias, the governor of Bethulia, was in a great quandary, and he called his ministers to him. "Now will these men [the Assyrians] lick up the face of the earth," he said, "for neither are the high mountains nor the hills able to bear their weight. Let us to prayer, brethren, and haply God will relieve us in this our woeful strait." No one, neither man nor woman, apparently, could see a way out of these dire circumstances.

Meanwhile, the Canaanites were advising Holofornes to make a raid upon the fountains of Bethulia, at the foot of the hill on which the city stood, in order to deprive the inhabitants of the town of their only water supply. Holofornes was taken with this plan, and dispatched his men to the fountains, where a superior number of Assyrians drove off the Israelites and cut off the supply of water. Suffering rose in Bethulia to such a pitch that the elders of the town approached Ozias and demanded that he surrender the Galilean bastion. The governor vacillated, and recommended five days of prayer; if before that time the God of Israel did not interpose, then he would surrender.

The last stores of water gave out, and the inhabitants fell fainting in the streets, and many died with each passing day. Matters stood in darkness, indeed, for the Bethulians, and hence for the Jewish nation and Jewish tradition as well.

We see, then, that the disparate elements in this biblical tale are brought together to form an ominous and heart-rending crisis for the Jews. And, as in the tales of Deborah and the woman of Abel, it seemed beyond the power of any man to take the measures necessary to bring matters to a successful resolution, when a woman's figure moved upon the stage to take charge, enact the will of the Lord, and deliver her people. That a pious and faithful widow, who quietly mourned her husband and diligently observed God's laws, rose to the position of leader and warrior among the Jews is not surprising. We have seen the fiery natures underlying the piety and calm surface of such women as Sarah, Rachel, Miriam, and Esther; and we know, too, that Mosaic institutions encouraged the independence and equality of the nation's women. Again and again Jewish women in the Old Testament are shown following their various occupations and then, whenever the law is transgressed or the nation imperiled, rising up without hindrance to voice their views and, if need be, to take the rudder of state directly into their hands. Judith was one such woman—indeed, she in some ways surpasses the heroines we have encountered. She was as militant as Miriam and as courageous as Deborah, and conbined in her person the quiet faith of Hannah and the shrewd intelligence of Esther.

Judith's soul was torn by the plight of her people, and yet enraged because the leaders were of such little faith. She knew how important was the strategic position of Bethulia in Israel's cause, and how vital that it be held. She thought deeply and decisively on the matter, and begged Ozias and his ministers to come to her house. She promised to reveal to them a way to save the city. In such high regard was the widow held that Ozias lost no time in gathering together his brethren and making his appearance before Judith.

"Hear me now, ye Governor of Bethulia!" said Judith to them. "The words which ye have spoken to the people this day, are not right touching this oath, that you have promised to deliver the city to our enemies, unless within these days the Lord turn and help you. And now, who are ye that have tempted God this day, to stand in the stead of God to the children of men?" In other words, Judith believed that they had no right to say that unless God intervened on the city's behalf before a certain time they would give up a sacred charge with which they had been entrusted. She told them it was their duty to stand by their posts and trust in God, and not place conditions upon him as to when or how he should help them.

"And now," she added, "try the Lord Almighty, and ye shall never know anything. For ye cannot find the depth of the heart of a man, neither can ye perceive what he thinketh; how, then, can ye search out God, that hath made all things, and comprehend His purposes? Nay, my brethren, provoke not the Lord our God to anger; for if He will not help within five days, He hath power to help us when He will, even every day. Do not bind the counsel of the Lord, for God is not a man that he may be threatened. Therefore, let us wait for salvation from Him, and call upon Him, and He will hear, if it please Him."

Then she pointed up the disgrace and national dishonor that would come upon them if they betrayed their trust and allowed the sacred inheritance, the newly recovered tabernacle, to be defiled and destroyed. And she ended her plea with an heroic exhortation: "Now, therefore, O brethren, let us show an example to our brethren, because their hearts depend on us, and the sanctuary and the house and the altar rest on us."

Ozias and the ministers replied, "Therefore, pray thou for us, for thou art a goodly woman, and the Lord will send us rain, and fill our cisterns that we thirst no more."

The governors were humbled by her words, and could see the truth in her view. They resolved not to sell their faith so cheap, or the endurance of the people so low, and agreed to resist, no matter what cost.

It was at that juncture that Judith was struck with a flash of inspiration. As the governors were taking their leave, she told them that if they sent her out into Holofornes's camp, the Lord would visit Israel by her hand. She asked that they not inquire any more of her, until she had thought further on the matter—a request to which the governors readily agreed.

After their departure, "Judith fell on her face, and put ashes on her head, and uncovered the sackcloth wherewith she was clothed, and about the time that the incense of that evening was offered in Jerusalem in the house of the Lord, Judith cried with a loud voice to the Lord."

Her prayer is on a par, in its simplicity and beauty, with that of Hannah. Indeed, there is the same devotion and all-abiding faith in her eloquence:

> Behold, the Assyrians are multiplied in their power, and are exalted with horse and man; they glory in the strength of their footmen; they trust in shield and spear and bow, and know not that Thou art the Lord that breakest battles. The Lord is Thy name. Throw down their strength in Thy power, and bring

down their force in Thy wrath, for they have purposed to defile Thy sanctuary, and to pollute the tabernacle where Thy glorious name resteth, and to cast down with sword the home of Thy altar. Behold their pride. Send Thy wrath upon their heads, and give unto me, which am a widow, the power that I have conceived. For Thy power standeth not in multitude, nor Thy might in strong men; for Thou art the God of the afflicted, Thou art an helper of the oppressed, an upholder of the weak, a protector of the forlorn, a savior of them that are without hope. I pray Thee, I pray Thee, O God my father, King of every creature! hear my prayer, and make my speech and deceit to be their wound and stripe, who have purposed cruel things against Thy covenant, and Thy hallowed house, and against the house of the possession of Thy children."

When her prayer was ended, Judith arose, and, having anointed herself, she plaited her hair, adorned it with jewels, and arrayed herself in one of her rich dresses, which she had not worn since the death of Manasses. Her feet were decorated with sandals of scarlet and gold; bracelets, chains, and rings, ornamented the rest of her person. She was a women renowned for her beauty, and now that she was adorned in her costliest garments, she might easily hope to attract the notice of the Assyrian general. For such, to be sure, was her plan—to go boldly into the Assyrian camp, deceive Holofornes, and then destroy him. She was dressed like a princess, but she was, in fact, a warrior, on her way to do dangerous and bloody deeds.

With a maid, Judith left the city and made her way towards the Assyrian camp, meaning to be taken prisoner. She was hailed by Assyrian sentries and halted in her tracks. They might easily have struck her down or ravaged her, but she boldly spoke up to them. "I am a Hebrew woman," she said. "I have fled from the city to the camp of Holofornes, to go before him, and show him a way to take the city, and pass through the hill country without the loss of a man."

A sensation was produced by her entrance into the Assyrian camp.

Then there was a concourse through all the camp, for her coming was noised among the tents, and they came about her as she stood waiting without the tent of Holofornes: and they wondered at her beauty, and admired the children of Israel because of her, and every one said to his neighbors, Who would despise this people that have among them such women?

It was now late evening, and Holofornes came from his tent, his servants bearing silver lamps before him. The general was struck with the woman's nobility and beauty, and he led her into his tent. Inside, he seated himself, and motioned to Judith to take a place next to him, but she threw herself at his feet, imploring his mercy and protection. The Assyrian commander, touched, told her to rise, saying, "Woman, be of good comfort; fear not in thy heart, for I will not hurt whosoever serveth King Nebuchadnezzar. If thy people that dwelleth in the mountains had not set light by me, I would not have lifted up my spear against them. Now, therefore, tell me, why art thou fled from them and come unto me?"

She told him that she had fled the city because famine and thirst had visited it. She told him further that the Canaanite prince whom he had expelled had spoken true, that the Jews were under the protection of their God so long as they did not violate the tenets of their religion. But because they were so sorely pressed by want, she told the general, they would surely transgress, and eat of the forbidden offerings of the altar. Thus God would turn against them.

"Now, then, my lord," she concluded, "be guided by me. Permit thine handmaid to go out in the plain each night to pray, and God will tell me when they have done this sin, and I will tell thee, then shalt thou go forth with thine army, and thou shalt have an easy victory."

Holofornes was astonished at all he heard. He thanked Judith for her offered services, and declared himself ready to act as she might dictate. Such passion burned in him at the sight of her that he said, "Fair Judith, thou art beautiful in thy countenance, and wit there is in thy words. Surely, if thou do as thou hast spoken, thy God shall be my God, and thou shalt dwell in the house of Nebuchadnezzar, and be renowned throughout the whole earth!"

The general installed Judith near his own tent, and gave her the right to exercise her own religion—such was the power of her beauty over him. And she had, of course, the right to come and go to and from the camp as she chose.

Some days were spent in this way, in which Judith went forth every evening for prayer and ablutions at the fountain. Then Holofornes called a feast, during which he designed to seduce the Jewess, as was his right, he felt, and her expectation. Judith had remained aloof from him, in her cunning way, and had only increased his lusts thereby. The woman bided her time, waiting for the moment to strike.

The invitation to the feast was extended to her by messenger of the general: "Let not this fair damsel fear to come unto my lord, and to be honored in his presence, and to drink wine and be merry, and to be made this day as one of the Assyrians that serve in the house of Nebuchadnezzar."

Judith graciously accepted the invitation, decked herself with all her jewelry, and, superbly attired, she entered the tent of the general and sat on a couch. The Assyrians gathered there wondered at her beauty, and Holofornes more than ever wished to possess her.

"Drink and be merry with us, Judith," said the general. "Be not afraid of me, for my heart is filled with love for thee. Thou art the fairest of women, O Judith."

"I will drink, now, my lord," said Judith, "because my life is magnified in me this day more than all the days since I was born."

Judith ate and drank the food her own maid had prepared—for she would not touch the idolator's repast—and so excited the Assyrian commander by her loveliness and wit that he drank more than he had been accustomed to, and Judith foresaw that he would be in a state befitting her purpose. When the feast was over, and the guests and captains departed, the servants closed the tent and left Judith alone with Holofornes, who was senseless with drink on the couch.

> Then all went out and there was none left in the bedchamber, neither little nor great. Then Judith, standing by the bed, said in her heart, O Lord God of all power, look, at this present, on work of my hands for the exaltation of Jerusalem. For now is

the time to help Thy inheritance and to execute my enterprise to the destruction of the enemies that are risen up against us. Then came she to the pillow of the couch, and took down the fauchion from thence, and approached his bed, and took hold of the hair of his head, and said, Strengthen me, O Lord God of Israel, this day, and she smote twice upon his neck with all her might, and she took away his head from him and went forth.

At Judith's signal her maid entered, who, tearing down the jeweled canopy, wrapped the head in it, and placed it in her bag. Folowing her mistress, they left the camp unmolested, as if for their usual prayer, and hastened to the gate of Bethulia.

Then called Judith afar off to the watchmen, Open now the gates, for God, even our God, is with us to show His power yet in Israel and His strength against the enemy.

The watchmen ran down joyfully to admit her, and brought her to an open space near the gate, where stood the governors and many of the city's inhabitants around a large watchfire.

Judith was, apparently, delirious: "Praise, praise, praise God, praise God, I say, for He has not taken away His mercy from the house of Israel, but hath destroyed the enemy by my hand this night."

Removing Holofornes's head from the bag, she exulted:

Behold the head of Holofornes, the chief captain of the army of Assyria, and behold the canopy where he did lie in his drunkenness, and the Lord hath smitten him by the hand of a woman. As the Lord liveth, who hath kept me in my way that I went, my countenance hath deceived him to his destruction, yet he hath not committed sin with me to defile and shame me.

Then Ozias said:

O daughter, blessed art thou among all the women of the earth, and blessed be the Lord God which created the heavens and the earth, which hath directed thee to the cutting off of the head of our chief enemy. For this thy confidence shall not depart from the hearts of men which remember the power of God forever. And God turn these things for a perpetual praise, because thou hast not spared thy life for the affliction of our nation, but hast avenged our ruin, walking in a straight way before God. And all the people said, Amen, so be it.

Judith accepted the homage of her governor and people, and related to them the details of all she had done since leaving the city. They carried her off to her house with all reverence.

When morning broke, Holofornes's head was hung upon the wall, and the Israelites assembled outside the gates. The Assyrian guards, watching this strange turn of events, went to inform Holofornes's captains. They then went to the tent of the commander, tore open the tent, and beheld with horror his headless corpse.

"Treason! treason!" they cried. "This Hebrew woman hath brought shame upon the house of Nebuchadnezzar. Holofornes is slain!"

Confusion prevailed in the Assyrian camp; in spite of the captains' best efforts to retrench, panic spread from rank to rank, and all the men rushed about in fear of the wrath of the Hebrew God. The entire camp broke and the regiments fled.

The inhabitants of Bethulia rushed out after them. Sending messengers to the hill forts around them, the people ran out, and soon the beleaguered Assyrians were assailed on all sides by the citizens of Bethomestham and Chobai and the people of the hill country and the seacoast.

When the bloodshed was over and the spoils taken, Israel was free.

Great was the joy in Jerusalem at the deliverance of the nation, and the name of Judith of Bethulia was upon every tongue, with terms of wonder and praise. To do her all possible honor, Joachim, the high priest, resolved to visit her, in order to give thanks on behalf of all the Israelites and sons of Judah.

Accompanied by a long train of priests and the great and good of Jerusalem, he arrived at Bethulia. Judith came forth to meet him, and knelt before him. Blessings were showered upon her by every voice.

"Arise, my daughter," said the high priest. "Thou art the exaltation of Jerusalem, thou art the great glory of Israel! thou art the joy and rejoicing of our nation. Thou hast done much good in Israel, with thy hand; and God is pleased therewith. Blessed be thou of the Almighty Lord forevermore." And all the people cried, "Amen!"

Judith then accompanied the procession back to Jerusalem. She had resolved to dedicate the spoils taken from the Assyrians to the glory of God at the tabernacle. And there, amidst pomp and splendor and heartfelt thanksgiving, she could contain herself no longer, and burst forth in a song of praise to the Lord God of Israel, a song that echoes the anthems of Miriam and Deborah. So wonderful is this song, so eloquent, and so illustrative of the truly exalted position of women in the Old Testament that we quote it here in full, as a fitting conclusion to the amazing, many-faceted gallery of scriptural women we have encountered.

The Assyrian came from the mountains of the north,
He came with ten thousands of armies.
The multitudes thereof stopped the torrents.
The horsemen covered the hills.

He bragged that he would burn up my border,
That he would kill my young men with the sword,
That he would dash the suckling children against the ground,
And make the children a prey and the virgins a spoil.

But the Almighty hath disappointed him by the hand of a woman!
The mighty one did not fall by young men,
Neither did the sons of Titans set upon him,
Nor did the high giants set upon him.

But Judith, daughter of Merari, weakened him with her beauty.
For the exaltation of the oppressed in Israel
She put off her garments of widowhood, anointed herself,
Bound her hair, and used raiments to deceive him.

Her sandals ravished his eyes,
Her beauty took his mind prisoner,
So the fauchion passed through his neck.
Thus will I sing unto my God a new song.

O Lord, Thou art great and glorious,
Wonderful in strength and invincible.
Let all creatures praise Thee,
For Thou speakest and they were made.

Thou sentest Thy spirit and created them.
There is none can resist Thy voice;
The mountains shall be moved from their foundations,
The rocks shall melt like wax at Thy presence.

Yet art Thou merciful to them that fear Thee,
For all sacrifice is too little for a sweet savor unto Thee,
All the fat is not enough for burnt-offerings—
But he that feareth the Lord is great at all times!